Gordon with his insight and knowledge of the science of psychology weaves between his own romance and his work with a patient with a love disturbance. The reader wonders how each will turn out. It is a great read for therapists, psychology students, patients or anyone who has both loved and lost or suffered the pains and confusion of romantic love." Gerd H. Fenchel, Ph.D. Dean/Director, Washington Square Institute for Mental Health and author of "Psychoanalytic Reflections on Love and Sexuality."

"Robert Gordon is a psychologist, psychoanalyst, author and speaker. And he is a man who understands the nature of love. Speaking from his heart and speaking from his fund of knowledge, he teaches the reader the difference between romantic love and the kind of love that sustains us over the years. If you are in love or searching for it, read this book and heed its wisdom!"

Daniel Gottlieb, Psychologist and Family Therapist, host of "Voices In The Family" (WHYY Radio) columnist Philadelphia Inquirer, author "Voices In The Family" and "Letters To Sam"

"This is a great book. The reader learns a lot about love, relationships, psychology, and the usefulness of psychoanalytic psychotherapy. Although I have been a psychologist for many years, I learned a lot from reading this book. This is a great achievement by Dr. Gordon. It is written so that both professionals and nonprofessionals can read it, and learn from it." Russell Eisenman, Ph.D. author of over 200 journal articles and 7 books in psychology.

I Love You Madly!
On Passion, Personality and Personal Growth

I Love You Madly!
On Passion, Personality and Personal Growth

Robert M. Gordon, Ph.D.

ISBN : 1-4196-2354-0
Library of Congress Control Number : 2006901103

To order additional copies, please contact us.
BookSurge, LLC
www.booksurge.com
1-866-308-6235
orders@booksurge.com

I Love You Madly!
On Passion, Personality and Personal Growth

*To My Beautiful Wife Alla- My Soul-mate,
Colleague And Best Friend*

CONTENTS

Acknowledgements

I want to thank my office manager Shelle Scheirer who has been a friend, professional and help for my book and for my practice. Special thanks to my manuscript proof readers and editors who devoted many hours to helping me despite their busy professional schedules: Margaret Alonso, Russell Eisenman, Arthur Katz, Lawrence Levitt and Antonina Vasnetsova.

Most of all I would like to thank the love of my life, my inspiration and my best editor, my wife Alla, to whom I dedicate this book.

N.B. I have complied with the American Psychological Association's Ethical Principles of Psychologists and Code of Conduct by using disguised and composite characters for all my case examples.

Introduction

The Mystery of Love

Romantic love starts as a delusion that usually fades in unromantic reality. But on occasion, romantic love evolves into a lasting love relationship.

For over thirty years, as a psychologist, family therapist and psychoanalyst, I have studied why some loves fade and others flourish. I want to tell you what I have learned from research, practice and my own personal experience. I want to show you how to have more satisfying love relations. I hope that reading this book will be as much a growth experience for you as writing it has been therapeutic for me.

I will show you that the course of love is relatively predictable based on the personalities and histories of the lovers. What will happen later in the relationship is evident from the very beginning. All the signs are there from the start.

My patient George had a hostile relationship with his alcoholic mother. He married young to escape her. He married an alcoholic woman. He divorced her and remarried. Alice, his second wife was also an alcoholic.

George protested when I suggested that he repeated his attachment with his mother in his love relations. George said, "Alice had stopped drinking before we first met. It was only after the second year of marriage that she began to drink again."

George's urge to repeat his attachment pattern was unconscious. I interpreted, "You knew she once had a drinking problem and you could have unconsciously detected many of her personality traits that were similar to your mother. Her traits triggered the feelings of idealization that you first had for your mother. This primitive idealization is the root of all love. That came long before any awareness of a conflict with your mother. When you fall in love, you would enact both sides of the emotions in your love relations, first idealization and then the old conflicts from childhood."

George was not ready to concede that he had a goal directed unconscious. "How is that possible? I saw her across the room at a party. It was love at first sight."

I explained, "The human face has about thirty muscles that can be used for emotional expression. They can communicate many subtle messages. Our unconscious can read aspects of a person's personality and emotions from the face (Young, 1997). You were attracted to the way she looked, her non-verbal expressions and then what she said. They were all triggers for your unconscious love drama."

Over the many psychotherapy sessions George began to see the patterns he was repeating in his relationships. Eventually he gained enough personal growth to love more wisely and develop passion for a much healthier woman.

The very act of falling in love sets in motion a fairly predictable course. I believe that everything people complain about later in their relationships is there from the start. People do not recognize problems consciously, but unconsciously they certainly do. Lovers begin with an overture that subtly introduces all the themes that are to come. These themes continue throughout the relationship. They build until they are resolved or until they destroy the intimacy.

Each love is a different experience. Yet a new love tends to enact old patterns of how we love. These patterns are set deep within our personalities.

We recreate our childhood attachments, traumas and conflicts in our intimate relationships. Our childhood perceptions of our parents, as idealized gods or as tormenting demons, became internal gyroscopes orienting us to lovers who evoke similar emotions in us. If we imprinted on a tormenting parent, then a tormenting lover will be exciting and a kind lover will seem boring. We can repeat our childhood relationships by unconsciously picking a lover who evokes similar emotions from childhood, or we can provoke or distort our lover in order to repeat an intimacy pattern.

Sometimes we are just confused as to how to even recognize or act to emotional problems in a lover, if dysfunctional relationships have been so much of our childhood experiences. The love drama is repeated over and over and sometimes the roles are interchangeable. If our lover is not the tormentor then we become the tormentor. But the love drama is the same, moving towards the same outcome. If our primary caregivers were negligent or traumatizing, you can predict that the outcomes of our later passions will tend to produce the same emotions.

If we had wonderful parents and have a secure identity, then romantic love usually evolves into lasting love. Many people are not so lucky. Many of us need to work hard to love wisely. The only way I know to alter a love conflict is through emotional insight in the context of a healthy intimacy.

All intimacies that promote personal growth have certain things in common: commitment, constructive feedback, emotional insight, concern, remorse, responsibility, and a willingness to be a better person. If these conditions are met in a love relationship, there can be personal growth.

However, most people avoid insight and seek an ideal love with a magical hero or heroine (Bergmann, 1982; Freud, 1914/1957). Falling in love is a return to the emotions of infancy when we felt a magical symbiosis with an idealized caregiver. In childhood our love matures with the interaction of healthy parents. With the continuing lessons of love that we can learn in a healthy family, we later can fall in love with a realistic appreciation of the beloved. With too much emotional trauma, an infantile notion of a magical love becomes fixated and gets repeated in adult love relations. Mature love requires the idealization of truth; romantic love requires the idealization of love itself.

The most reliable corrective intimacy is psychotherapy. But intense love can also be a great motivator. A lover may become a better person for the sake of the relationship. I will illustrate this by telling you about a psychotherapy case, and a case of intense romantic love. I will take you inside the psychotherapy of one of my patients, Karen, sharing with you how I treated her self-defeating problems with love.

I will also take you inside the mind of a psychologist in love. I will tell you about my relationship with Alla. Although, I have never suffered from a serious mental illness, I have known the delusions of romantic love. And with one foot in passion and the other in psychology, I will use myself as an example.

Psychotherapists keep their personal lives away from patients for good reasons. Patients use the therapeutic relationship as a symbolic one to work through emotional problems. The psychotherapist comes to represent in patients' minds their mother, father or bad self. Whatever is conflicted and unfinished will be placed on to the psychotherapist. Telling stories about my life may be a disruption of the patient's deep work. However, in the context of a book, I think it is useful to show the reader that anyone can fall into the madness of romantic love and how knowledge of psychology can help.

All people, including psychologists can lose perspective when they fall in love, no matter how mature and informed. However psychology can provide a useful road map when one becomes lost in emotions. As I tell the story of my relationships with Alla and Karen, I will explain the psychology of passion, personality and personal growth.

The science of psychology is not presented in these case studies but rather in the presentation of the psychological theories and research in the context of story. I have created these characters from combinations of patient's traits, histories and psychotherapy notes. I put privacy as a main consideration in this narrative non-fiction.

We are all self-deluding historians. Now as I take a deeper look back, wisdom arrives. We can all love madly. But personal growth comes from self-reflection and insight. <u>We can all</u>

grow to love better by learning from and not rationalizing our mistakes.

Although Alla and Karen come from different worlds, they both struggle with similar conflicts about love. When I confronted each of them with insights about themselves, they were faced with a decision about giving up their defensiveness or giving up on love. We all make choices to learn from our mistakes or to become defensive. These choices affect the quality of our lives more than anything else we do. Join me in my stories of Alla and Karen and learn from them why some loves fade and others flourish.

Chapter 1

The Attraction Stage

During the last days of August several years ago, I began my article on romantic love. I had time to write without disruption except to see my patients.

"Ziv's research (1993) suggests four stages of romantic love:
1. The Attraction stage (looks interesting),
2. The Examination stage (closer look at the surface facts),
3. The Self Revealing stage (deeper look at personality) and
4. The Mutual Expectation stage (how well the relationship works in dealing with the practical tasks of life).

The Attraction stage of romantic love is a reaction to concrete triggers, such as physical characteristics. This initial attraction is based on fantasies and little of the reality of the person. Infatuation lives outside the realm of reality and is therefore wonderfully magical. It begins as a dream to make up for losses and often ends up repeating them. Romantic love is a joyous delusional state."

I had been divorced for several years. I had 50% custody of my children. Now they were both off to college. I was alone. I now had time to work on my paper about the mystery of love relations. I had been working on this issue since my Ph.D. dissertation. But now it seemed not just theoretical, but also personally useful. I felt it was time to marry again.

While I searched the Internet for articles on love, I saw an ad for meeting women in Eastern Europe. I had seen it before and wondered how anyone could possibly date someone thousands of miles away. Long distance relationships are filled in with fantasy and not the test of real life situations. Far away lands may symbolize far-fetched dreams.

But this particular woman in the banner ad was impossible to ignore. I had to stop and stare at her face.

The research of evolutionary psychologists indicates that at the most basic level men instinctively wish to mate with youthful, fertile-looking women and women wish to mate with men with attributes of power, security and resources (Buss, 1994; Eisenman, 2001a)

But biological forces are just one factor. Other factors modify this primitive urge. Our temperaments affect our attractions. Opposites attract because we look to others to have our needs met. We might fall in love with someone who possesses something we feel we lack, or provides a complement to our personality. A nurturing person and an insecure person may be attracted to one another.

But while opposites may attract, relationships are easier to maintain when both partners share the same frame of reference. Happily married couples have elements of both similarity and opposite traits. They have similar values and goals in life and yet fill in for each other's personality (Richard, 1990; Winch, 1958).

Imprinting on our primary care givers and family dynamics add to the chemistry (Dicks, 1967; Kernberg, 1995). We fall in love with people who evoke feelings similar to those that characterized our first attachments. These associations are stored in the primitive part of our brain without cognition or conscious memory.

Cultural beliefs and recent love experiences add to feelings of attraction (Aron and Aron, 1989). A person may feel attraction or repulsion based on a recent experience. Certain situations may leave a person vulnerable to falling in love.

The more mature the love, the more a person's values, good qualities and goals contribute to passion. A less mature love is based more on concrete triggers that have no bearing on a lasting satisfying love.

Instincts, temperament, family experiences, beliefs and recent experiences were all factors operating in my unconscious. They all combined to produce fantasies of a romance with this woman in the ad. I was in the first stage of delusion. Then I wondered if she was a professional model used to encourage sales. I went back and forth between reason and erotic fantasy. I clicked on her photo and found more pictures of her. The professional looking photos showed a vivacious young woman with short dark hair, high cheekbones, large brown almond-shaped eyes and long slender legs.

Her name was Alla, and her ad stated that she was a 30-year-old fashion designer from Saint Petersburg, Russia. She was 5 foot 7, 117 pounds. She had a Ph.D. in literature. Alla listed her interests as psychology, philosophy, music, literature, art and fashion.

Now for the first time in my life, I was free. I could go anywhere and have an adventure. Why not? So, I wrote to her. She seemed so unreal; I never expected anything to come of it.

I wrote: "Dear Alla, It's great to see that you are also interested in psychology. I am a 52-year-old Jewish psychologist. I am looking for a sweet woman who is easy going, not defensive, and without psychological problems that interfere with a healthy intimacy..." I went on shamelessly selling myself while attempting to sound humble. I enclosed my photo and the link to my web site.

For a day or two, I enjoyed fantasies about an exciting international romance with a gorgeous young woman. But it soon faded as I realized how unrealistic the whole thing was.

A few weeks later, I sat with my morning coffee and read the online news about the recent terrorist attacks.

I then went to my email. I choked on my coffee. I saw, "From: Alla". It was the gorgeous woman from the banner ad! My fantasy stepped out of an evening's musing and responded.

Date: Sept. 26
From: Alla
To: Robert
Subject: Let me please introduce myself. My name is Alla.
Dear Robert,
I received your letter today (5 days ago I was in Italy, 2 days ago in Moscow, my ship of dizzy adventures brought me back to Saint Petersburg...my home-town...)

First, I want to say, I really regret the American tragic news. The Russian people empathize with the Americans so much. Tears fill my eyes when I think about the innocent victims.

Now...(my Russian time 0.34 a.m.) I am listening to Diane Schuur (song—"Easy Living") and I drink coffee with milk. I am reading W. Blake and some Haiku, violet loneliness. It is a perfect cocktail, the Japanese poetry and the lovely, great voice of the singer.

If to tell you the truth, today I have an extraordinary romantic mood, and this lunar instability doesn't make me nervous.

My best friends have left this country. My luxuriant intellectual conversations with my friends have faded and have become pale.

Do you like Heidegger, Kafka, or Herman Hesse?...I just wonder, maybe you like more Sartre, Nietzsche, or Mikhail Bulgakov?

I feel very privileged to get your attention...(especially taking into account your accomplishments...I saw your web site...).

I also have no trouble meeting intelligent, charming, and good-looking men...(smile without end).

Anyway, it was great to see someone interested in psychology.

So..... What about me?

(Brief if not so tiresome description for you): Alla has very high self-esteem, never pessimistic, stimulated with life's activities, tolerant of the religious beliefs and practices of others, extroverted, assertive and gregarious.

Alla doesn't have deep fears, paranoid delusions, hallucinations, and somatic complaints.

I am almost always self-confident, competitive, insightful, sensitive, and rational.

Sometimes I can be overly sensitive.

However, I cannot find people with whom I can discuss my mad, spiritual, ironic ideas. They do not share the various forms of my imagination.

They do not share the acrid smoke of my opinions and don't understand the artifacts of my individuality. Maybe, my weird, dizzy style is too complicated for them. I am very much the intellectual, artistic type and a deep thinker.

I do dream a lot (a problem?), but it's tempered with realistic expectations. In my own evaluation of myself, my flaws are obvious to me. When some people look at me, they envy me to some degree...They see that I'm successful...They see my 'happy face' (my good mask...). What they fail to see, what they can't see, what's behind the mask...

Maybe this is just a standard deficiency of a "thinking person"? What do you think, Robert?

What are you looking for? What type of woman?

Do you want to discover my inner true treasures? You said: "Your intelligent and beautiful eyes intrigued me." hmm...(An innocent smile of Buddha).

You have great intuition and you are right.

I know about psychoanalytic psychotherapy, and complex psychopathology. I studied Psychoanalysis (and many other wise and interesting theories)...Maybe, some day, I would like to study at your institute. I need a sponsor anyway. (Big smile)

What do you think about the maturational level of my personality, I just wonder?...Maybe already you think that I need some therapy (Smile). Maybe, I sound foolish (and look like a UFO on the Internet...)

Are you interested in the delicate facets of my delightful personality? Do you want to explore this face to face (SMILE)?

Best wishes,

Alla.

She looked beautiful and accomplished in her ad, and her email revealed a charming and clever personality. Alla enclosed a photo of her beautiful eyes since I had commented on them in my letter. This was the sort of woman I had seen in fashion ads. She was sort of woman men dream about. I indulged in a fantasy, never expecting a reply. Now what do I do?

Chapter 2

Disturbances in Love Relations

Otto Kernberg (1974, 1976, 1980, 1995) wrote of two basic love pathologies found in the most disturbed individuals: the inability to fall in love and the inability to remain in love. Salman Akhtar (1999) added three more love disturbances: the tendency to fall in love with the "wrong" kinds of people, the inability to fall out of love and the inability to feel loved.

The most severe form of love disturbance is the inability to fall in love. In order to fall in love some degree of idealization or overvaluing is necessary. In normal love the idealization is primarily based on real qualities. In pathological cases the idealization is extreme and can become delusional with an equal but opposite devaluation lurking beneath. However people who cannot fall in love at all either cannot feel an idealization of another or the idealization is a fickle and fleeting fantasy.

Individuals may have problems falling in love because:

1. they are egocentric. They lack the capacity to love another.

2. They dread closeness since closeness is associated with the destruction of their fragile psychological world.

The next level of disturbance is when a person can fall in love but cannot remain in love. Personalities that fall into this category have the capacity for idealization and erotic desire. They unconsciously seek a magical love that is worthy of their grandiose self and also a rescuer that is transformational.

However, they experience a great deal of hostility when the idealized love object does not live up to the hoped for magical transformation. They may become obsessed with deficiencies in the love object. They often fear that intimacy will reveal that they are a fraud and may project this on to the love object and come to see the formally idealized lover as a fraud. A cycle of idealization and devaluation of the other moves the person in and out of closeness. There is no true intimacy with a real person. Love is a child's fantasy. They fall in love with a fantasy and then punish the real person for not obeying the fantasy.

Individuals may evolve from not being able to fall in love, to being able to fall in love but not remain in love. They might fall in love with the "wrong people" in service to their unconscious need to not remain in love.

"Why was he wearing gloves?" I asked after looking at the photographs.

The coroner explained, "It's not gloves. It's his skin. After a few days of his hanging there, the hands get dark from the pooled blood in them...we want to know if it was a suicide or a murder made to look like a suicide."

We ordered lunch at the deli in my office building as I studied the photographs, documents that included the deceased's psychiatric history, interviews from people who knew him and a statement from the woman he mentioned in his suicide note.

I sometimes do a psychological autopsy in my role as a forensic psychologist. A strange role when combined with my roles as a research psychologist and psychoanalyst. Actually, they all go together since they all are about weighing evidence to solve a mystery of one sort or another.

I looked up and said, "The records show that he suffered from paranoid schizophrenia. He had been hospitalized for it several times. The suicide note is consistent with his delusions. I also see a consistency between his previous writings and the suicide note. He felt that he could never have the woman of his delusional love. He may have killed himself to both stop his suffering and to punish her."

The detective said, "She lives in the same building, but she never had a relationship with him. No one has ever seen him with any woman. I don't understand."

"Romantic love is delusional state. For normal people romantic love is only a temporary delusion that is more kind than cruel. It's usually cruel for people with a psychosis. He was psychotic. He didn't have the ability to fall in love with a real person. He wouldn't be able to perceive reality enough to love or remain in love. What's the real reason for calling me in on this? You must know it was a suicide and not a murder."

The coroner and detective looked at each other and the coroner said, "His family is Catholic and they are contesting my assessment of suicide. They think he was murdered."

I thought out loud, "And you want a psychological autopsy to back you up? But by saying it's a suicide his family would be deprived of the belief that his soul can rest in heaven. Gentlemen, this is a matter of interacting systems. The system inside the deceased's mind was a delusional love that finally broke him. The legal system needs to give a determination of the death, which is suicide. He was also part of a family and religious system where suicide is a mortal sin."

The coroner and detective nodded.

I continued my formulation which was a combination of psychoanalysis, forensic psychology and systems theory. "I think I can help you and the family. Ironically, his diagnosis could save his soul. If he killed himself in a psychotic state he would have not used free will. He would not be culpable under canon law. He might be able to have a Church funeral and burial."

The detective said, "Which Catholic school did you attend?"

I laughed, "I went to Hebrew school. To be sure, I'm going to check with my psychologist monk friend Dr. Bernard Seif."

The Coroner said, "But I still don't understand something. How can he have killed himself over someone he never even met?"

"She was only a screen for his projected fantasies. He was probably afraid of a real relationship and may have needed an idealized delusional love to make up for his misery. The more unhappy a person is, the more that person looks for someone to fill in the empty spaces inside. Possibly when that failed to work, he fell into a total demoralization and self-destruction."

We finished our lunch, and I promised them a written report in about a week. I walked around the building so I could climb the stairs to my office on the third floor. It was late summer and the air was beginning to get cooler. The image of that man hanging by a rope alone for days in his apartment stayed with me. Away from my professional demeanor, I felt the sadness of it all. So many people suffer from a tragic love affair. Some become crushed and wither. Some go over the edge. So many crimes are committed in the name of love. Some murder or commit suicide over what they think is love. It is not about love, it is about not having enough of a self to weather the loss.

As I came into my waiting room, I saw Karen. I enjoy doing psychoanalytic psychotherapy. Even after many years, it still stimulates me intellectually and emotionally. I am lucky to have such meaningful and rewarding work. But some patients try to drive me crazy while I try to drive them sane. Karen felt empowered by defeating me. She saw her defensiveness as a strength.

Karen changed therapists the same way she changed men.

She starts out expecting magic and when she doesn't get it, she devalues the person. She had been in and out of psychotherapy of one sort or another (some bizarre) since she was a teenager. She came to therapy quoting several self-help books to help her find a man. She particularly liked advice that was deceptive and manipulative. That made sense to her. She justified her dishonesty since she assumed that men were innately untrustworthy.

Karen moaned, "Dr. Gordon, I came back to you because I tried everything else."

"It's been about four years. You didn't seem happy with me before." I said.

"I don't believe in Freud and going into the past."

Karen was really saying, "Help me, but don't ask me to look at myself." People who don't believe in Freud have probably not read or understood much of what he really said. His theories warn that people pay a price for lying to themselves. Defensive people don't like to hear that.

Karen, now 39, never married. Her love relationships rarely lasted more than a few months. The longest was with a married man for two years. When he broke it off, Karen got depressed. That's when I first saw her. She stayed a few months. When she fell in love again, she left therapy.

Karen's blue eyes scanned my face for hints of my feelings about her. She had punky short blond hair and several earrings on each ear. Karen was still skinny like a teen and dressed like one. She could easily attract a man and become infatuated for a while. Karen often picked low functioning men. Her rationalization was that she could have more control and she hoped they would appreciate her. But Karen picked low functioning men mainly so that it would be easy for her to devalue them and eventually reject them. When she found a man who treated her well, she would feel less passion and become demanding, dependent, provoke fights and blame the boyfriend for the conflicts.

Karen noticed my dog Roy who remained behind my chair.

"Your dog looks depressed. It's no wonder since he has to listen to all this crap."

"Karen, what can I do for you?" I asked. Karen was depressed and was projecting her feelings on to my dog. Karen transferred on to me that I wouldn't be able to tolerate her crap. Little did she realize how much she was showing me about herself already.

"I want you to help me find a man," Karen demanded.

"I'm an analyst not a matchmaker" I said clarifying my role.

"I keep picking jerks," Karen shrugged innocently.

"What do you want?"

"After the attacks on the 11th...I don't want to be alone...I want to be married."

"Not happily married?"

Karen was not ready for an interpretation. An interpretation is a translation from unconscious language to conscious language. Dreams, slips of the tongue, psychological symptoms, and relationship conflicts are all forms of unconscious language. Interpretation helps a person develop self-reflection. Self-reflection can mediate the expression of toxic emotions and self-defeating behaviors.

The recent psychological context of the terrorist attacks on 9.11 made Karen feel extra vulnerable. She wanted love to protect her. She wanted to be the cared for child and her man would be an undemanding ideal parent. I could have interpreted that the real reason Karen didn't say, "Happily married" was because it wasn't consistent with her conflicted attachment style. Her history with men proved this.

Right from the beginning, I saw many of the themes to come. I saw her problems with attachment by how she treated me.

An interpretation goes into forbidden territory into a person's most private place. I never go there without an invitation. For now, in this first phase of treatment, I made no deep interpretations; rather I clarified our roles and tasks.

"If you want me to help you to have a healthy intimacy, you

must allow yourself to have a therapeutic relationship with me. It will take emotional honesty, time and commitment."

Karen said, "I don't have the time and money. They don't pay nurses what they should."

Karen felt entitled to happiness. She didn't understand that she had to earn it.

"Your time and money will go to other things that will not affect your life as profoundly as psychotherapy."

"Sure. Sure." Karen sneered in a dismissive tone.

An emotionally corrective relationship could help a person have better intimacy. Psychotherapy is the most reliable method. But here is the irony; one needs to have the capacity for intimacy to form a therapeutic relationship to start with. It takes a good patient to get to the good therapy.

What does it take to be a good patient in psychotherapy?
1. a commitment to the therapeutic relationship,
2. openness to constructive feedback,
3. emotional insight into one's own flaws,
4. a capacity for concern and remorse,
5. a sense of responsibility for one's actions and situation in life, and
6. a willingness to be a better person.

If a patient can't do these things, there is no deep psychotherapy. There can be no increased ability for self-reflection and self-soothing. There is no increased ability for healthy love.

"Can you help me?" Karen demanded.

I reminded Karen of the protective boundary and ground rules of the therapy. Karen knew them, but like many patients, she would test the limits to see if I was trustworthy and professional. Karen had internal chaos. She brought chaos to her relationships. The structure and limits of the therapy might help her develop more structure and cohesion within her personality.

"I lease a regular time for you out of my practice. You are financially responsible for this leased time. We start on time and end on time. There are strict privacy rules. This firm boundary and commitment will intensify the treatment. I can't help you with intimacy without reproducing a therapeutic commitment..." As I went on to explain the details of the ground rules, Karen grew impatient.

"I know you have control problems," Karen said.

"If you come regularly and work hard you will probably have improvement."

"How much?"

Research shows that psychotherapy interventions are highly effective. But the main factors that lead to improvement are the personality qualities of the patient and the therapist and their relationship (Wampold, 2001). I need to have a healthy capacity to empathize with my patients. My empathy is often expressed in the tone, timing and accuracy of the therapeutic interventions. I apply the interventions as paint from a palette. I mix and apply as needed the right amounts of listening, questioning, clarifying, confronting, interpreting and reconstructions.

Mostly, I am silent when I work, actively listening to my patients. My silence in a safe atmosphere promotes a sense of autonomy and self-reflection in the patient. It also allows me to form a deep understanding of what the patient is trying to unconsciously communicate. (It is hard to show how silence works in writing. In reality, I did a lot of listening that is not evident in this story.) My empathic listening provides a psychological container for the patient's emotions. When patients cannot tolerate their affects, they can be laundered in our bi-personal field. They internalize my reactions and learn to better self-reflect, regulate their affects and self-sooth.

When an infant fusses, a mothering figure holds, launders and helps to contain the child's emotions (Bion, 1962a). Children internalize this early emotional environment in their implicit unconscious memory. Research has found that a person's capacity for self-reflection, affect regulation, self-soothing and a core self-concept evolves from this early interaction. These infant attachment and brain studies have lead to a reformulation of treatment. We now believe more than ever that working with affects in an empathic relationship is one of the most important growth factors in psychotherapy (Fonagy, 2002). If I intervene out of my own discomfort with the patient's emotions and just focus on symptom relief, I am not acting as a good container. Seeing Karen's problems in terms of her symptoms would reinforce her assumption that she is unknowable.

I use questions to take a patient deeper into personality. Questions may be used to get more information necessary for an interpretation or a reconstruction. Clarifications help improve reality testing, so that a patient might not continue operating on assumptions that are irrational or false.

When a patient is considering acting out in a destructive manner, there is often no time for an interpretation aimed at developing a more mature personality. I use confrontation to remind the patient of the consequences of acting out.

Interpretations of unconscious transferences, defenses, resistances and conflicts promote more insight and psychological maturity. Reconstruction of repressed areas of a patient's life helps develop a more cohesive sense of self. Reconstructing an emotional history can help patients make sense out of their symptoms and relationships.

I can never know a patient's true history. But having a sense of a continuous self that was built over time and can continue to grow over time is an important insight. Reconstructions allow a person to master problems that could not have been understood, tolerated or resolved earlier in life.

Almost everyone can benefit from venting in a supportive atmosphere. Most people find that the therapist's questions, clarifications, confrontations and even suggestions help them with symptom reduction. But a psychoanalytically informed psychotherapist is specifically trained to use interpretations and reconstructions to promote an actual maturation in personality structure.

Freud's goal of psychoanalysis was to achieve a profound growth of the mind so that the person can work and love better. Interpretations and reconstructions of the unconscious self-defeating side of personality are key ingredients to such profound changes.

Unfortunately, interpretations and reconstructions are frequently of limited value with patients who are concrete in their thinking and have little insight. For those individuals, cognitive-behavioral interventions that are symptom-focused may be more effective. These interventions are similar to the psychoanalytic interventions of questioning, clarifying and confronting.

There are few psychotherapists inclined to devote an extra five years of post doctoral work in training and their own psychoanalysis required for a specialization in psychoanalysis. There are few patients willing to put in the time and money for anything more than surface symptom relief. Psychoanalysis would then seem to be a dying art and science. But with a growing body of neuropsychoanalytic research to support it (Schore, 2003), psychoanalysis has become one of the largest divisions of the American Psychological Association. I have found that with every patient a psychoanalytic formulation is useful in helping me to understand what symptoms mean in the context of the whole person (McWilliams, 1994, 1999).

I understood Karen's off-putting defenses. She was scared. She had an insecure attachment style probably due to traumas in her childhood (Ainsworth, 1978; Bowlby, 1982; McCarthy and Taylor, 1999). Karen felt it is best to trust no one, pretend to be self-sufficient, demand intimacy but avoid it.

In this initial stage of treatment (Howard, 1996), the first thing to do is to give a patient hope that things can get better. When patients come into treatment they are often demoralized. When Karen said at the beginning of the session, "Dr. Gordon, I came back to you because I tried everything else," she was telling me how demoralized she was. She did not want a therapeutic relationship with me. She didn't believe that anything good could come from a committed intimacy. She thought that if she stayed too long in a relationship, she would be disappointed and hurt. Karen came back only after all else failed. But she wanted a magical cure.

The next phase of treatment often is about reducing symptoms, learning new skills and insights. That can happen in a few sessions to a few months. But her problem was not about a lack of skills. It was a deep fear of intimacy that was most likely based on a damaged self and trauma from childhood. But Karen did not want to go there.

Few patients stay long enough to go into the third phase of psychotherapy, the reconstructive phase of treatment and have personal growth. It could take years to change personality traits in order for a person to have personal growth and a better capacity for healthy love (Gordon, 2001; see figure 1; and also, Monsen, 1995). Reconstructive treatment such as that found in psychoanalytic psychotherapy, requires the patient to form an intimate alliance with the therapist and to self-reflect. I did not think that Karen could do that. She was too defensive for it. I would never tell Karen that. Karen needed to think that the answers to her problems would come from an idealized rescuer. She was waiting for her messiah.

I said, "How much improvement you make depends on what you put into it. I will need to see you twice a week to start, otherwise we will not get deep enough to change personality traits."

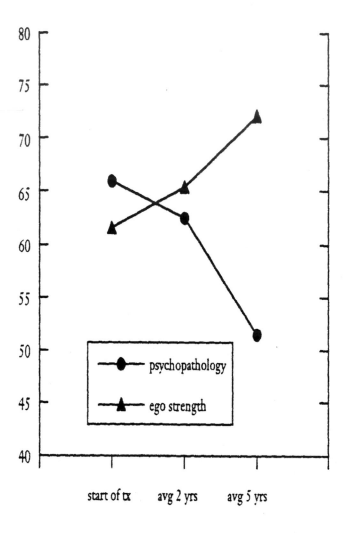

Figure 1: Changes in 55 patients as measured by the MMPI/

MMPI-2 (an objective test of psychopathology traits that are typically stable for years). Patients on average needed at least two years of psychoanalytic psychotherapy to begin to make profound changes to their personalities. They continued making changes in not only symptom relief but also in personal growth into their 5th year of treatment and beyond. The MMPI/MMPI-2 is non-reactive to short term treatments. The overall psychopathology was measured by scale A. The Ego strength scale was used to measure maturity (T45-55 represents normal scores, T65 and above are high scores). (Gordon, R.M. 2001; reprinted with permission from Issues in Psychoanalytic Psychology).

Chapter 3

The Examination Stage

I usually worked on my paper on love relations after office hours until about midnight and throughout the weekends. I was both writing about it and going through it at the same time.

"In the Examination stage of romantic love, people see how well they match in such areas as intelligence, interests, values and emotional compatibility. However, the accuracy of the data is confounded by the prospective lovers trying to sell themselves."

Date: Sept. 25 (This date is one day before Alla's letter. Saint Petersburg, Russia is 8 hours ahead of Pennsylvania.)
From: Robert
To: Alla
Subject: Hello Alla.

Dear Alla,
Thank you for your sympathy all the way from Russia. I just got back from New York City. Only jet fighters circled the sky over Manhattan and around the dark smoke that poured out of the ruins where about 20,000 people worked. We don't know how many thousands died. My country will never be the same.

As I wrote, I am a Jewish psychologist. I'm not sure what you know of Jews. Jews are a world people from an ancient race, that 3000 years ago had the abstract reasoning to imagine a God as a moral force rather than an idol. Jewish philosophy is that God started creation and we are to finish it. That is one reason why Jews are more into worldly things like science, art, law, medicine, and commerce, rather than concern for the afterlife. I'm not religious, but I appreciate the heritage and values of my people. My interest in psychoanalysis is an extension of my Jewish values of learning and self—reflection.

(I wanted to share my beliefs and values to see if we were compatible. Enough, on to flirting.)

I am so excited about you! So beautiful and brilliant. Brains and passion.

Thank you for your invitation to meet. I am willing to go anywhere to meet an extraordinary woman such as yourself.

(But I'm not ready yet to jump on a plane to Russia.)

I'll be in Jamaica at the end of November. I'd send you tickets. I'll put you up at a lovely resort and we can get to know each other. What is your phone number? (Down boy—you'll scare her away.)

(So much for restraint.)

Yours,

Robert

Date: Sept. 27

From: Alla

To: Robert

Subject: Buddhist meditations mixed with a healthy dose of common sense

Dear Robert,

I am so happy to hear from you. I have met several men

through the Internet service, many of them smart and kind, but...something still missing.

I am dreaming of a man wise and trustworthy...a man careful and kind; a man sensual and hot; a man romantic and caring; a man with humor and understanding so that I can have fun with him; a man intelligent so that I can be understood; a man worthy of my love...a knight, harmonious inside and outside...I want to save his individuality.

(I'm with her so far, but what is this about, "I want to save his individuality"?)

I need depth, passion and care, a native harbor for the ships of my dreams...I am a sparrow that has been shot at. I am a Taurus, Robert. I am a bull that participated in a bullfight. (Smile)

(What does this mean?)

I am a knowing old bird and I can to go through fire and water...I am not a Jewess. (Alas?) But I have Jewishness in my soul. (This soul was born 3000 years ago...)

(Is Alla part Jewish?)

I am emotionally mature and I can allow to myself Buddhist meditations mixed with a healthy dose of common sense not only on Sundays.

(Open-minded philosophy.)

I am the sort who will go anywhere to get just what I want. (I never get enough)

(Never enough? Uh Oh.)

How I love a smart man! Brains and passion! O-lala!!!

Words...Words...Even tons of words are only one drop in the ocean...It's nothing sometimes...I do not believe words any more...

(We need words for understanding.)

I believe actions in real life. (It's more wise, isn't it?)

I have removed my ad 2 months ago...how could you have found me?? By the way...it's strange...And about my work?

People say that I am a good professional. I have my Ph.D. and many skills…I love and need to be around beauty…Do you want to know more about it? No?

You said: Jamaica? Hhhmmm…sounds not bad…I've never been there…Though I adore Europe more…

I am VERY tired of life in Russia. (down girl, you'll scare him away.)

(Sounds like Alla is ready to leave Russia. Is she looking for a way to get out? Will her rescuer be appreciated after she no longer needs him for that role?)

Be inspired my stranger in the night…

Alla and I emailed each other about who we were and what we wanted. At first we worked on impressing each other with our intelligence and knowledge. We discussed poetry, literature, philosophy and of course psychology. But when she told me that she was never satisfied with her relationships, "I never get enough", it was a red flag to me.

Dependent people who are too proud to admit that they are dependent say that it is never enough. They express their dependencies by being demanding. They cannot feel contentment and they expect contentment to be supplied by others. When they remain unhappy, they assume it is the fault of the other person. They are insatiable.

But this was only a red flag amidst so much good. Everyone has some degree of psychological baggage. Besides Alla sent a photo that had appeared on a magazine cover. She had worked as a model before going for her Ph.D. She looked even more beautiful in this photo than in the photos she used in her ad. In most of her e-mails, Alla enclosed photos of herself. Not only did her beauty amaze me, but also how different she looked in each photo. Her hair color from photo to photo was various shades of brown, red, blond, or black. It was long, short, every possible style. She seemed to have many beautiful faces. She was queen, punk, innocent child, siren, fashion model, and more. I never saw anyone look so different. She radiated energy, sexuality and intelligence.

Date: Sept. 27
From: Alla
To: Robert
Subject: Let me please re-introduce myself. My name is Alla Artemova

Knock-knock...
I know...the visit of my person is not designated in your business schedule. But I am here. May I come in?

O, Lord...I thought the agency already had removed my stupid old ad! You bought a cat in a sack...
(Already Alla was telling me that I have bought her. This was also a warning that I might not understand what I had bought.)
Many months ago I had written the questionnaire with such scant information. It was at the urging of my mother. I did not want to be a White Crow, but I was extremely curious! And here you are! (Smile after smile)
Do you want to read my poems, to see my paintings, designs, photographs, and work for movies or TV, or to read the last scandalous interview with me? Or do you just want to hear my voice? (Smile)
(Alla enclosed her entry in the Saint Petersburg "Who's Who". It listed her degrees, certificates, and accomplishments in literature, poetry, music, fashion design, modeling, painting, photojournalism, teaching, and her work on T.V.)
Robert you wrote: "You never get enough? When you are enough, the world seems enough. Then there is contentment.

There is no perfect mate that can magically repair the self. That is for each of us to do ourselves. Alla, you seem frustrated with words. You are an artist with words. Words can transform solitary experiences into shared worlds..."

Oh, Lord. Beautiful stanza...Encore! Encore!

Sometimes, wise words are as strong as a high-quality drug! O, sweet Mantra. (Verba movent, exempla trahunt!...I like Latin...)...I am just haughty, nestling (ex plumis cognoscitur avis), ecstatic larva, simply a multicolored molecule close to you.

(Impressive.)

I am afraid to speak with you by phone...My colloquial English is weak still...I don't want to illustrate my dull, unspeakable ignorance...I bet you need perfect, hot, intellectual fuel for your extraordinary brain, my precious friend.

(What a dance of modesty and ego.)

Robert, people named me "The Rare Orchid In Life's Basket Of Blooms."

(Alla must have affected friends.)

Do you see the golden fleece of my Odyssey, Robert? Who are you in my life for this current existence? Sometimes, I think, I am 1000 years old, my dear...but people think I am sweet baby + crazy Artistic Type + a donor of a solar energy.

I like:

To go against the stream (zealous wild Amazon)

To call things by their names

To be first violin...Et sic de ceteris...

To shout at all crossroads: "I exist! Love me!" so...what about you, Dr. Gordon? (Smile) Who knows the confidential code of your soul?

You asked me if I did the photo of my "amazing eyes"?

I sometimes work as a fashion photographer...But this photo of my eyes—is not my work. Maybe, you want to see all my photos?

(Definitely.)

I can send for you my professional publications, my articles for magazines and articles about me, but they are in Russian... unfortunately...my modest stock of so-called successes is only 1% from your grand activity and popularity, my guru...I don't want to compete with you...you are a pro. You are on top. I'm not.. yet...

("My guru"? I love the sound of that. No I don't think it's ridiculous at all.)

I saw the list of your publications on your Web site, and I would want to read some of your articles...May I ask your permission to do it? How can I do it, Robert? I'm especially interested in:

1. Systems-Object Relation's View of Marital Therapy: Revenge and Reraising.

And

2. Love: The Most Important Ingredient in Happiness.

I would want to know about Love and Marriage. (I am hungry for your harmonious, bright, inspired words.) After all, I know nothing.

("I know nothing." I will later learn the significance of this.)
Be inspired, Robert.
I leave you for now.

Sept. 27
From: Robert
To: Alla
Subject: Psychology of Love

Dear Alla,
You are surprised that your ad is still there after you told them to take it out? I don't see it as destiny but as business. Why would they take your ad off? You are great advertising. You are such a beautiful, impressive woman. Many men have sent in their money hoping to marry you.

You asked about the confidential code to my soul. I'm American. We don't think much of confidential codes beyond our Internet passwords. Defenses just get in the way of intimacy. Maybe Russians needed such protection from their government.

But I know my code and content. I loved my 5-year, 4-day-a-week psychoanalysis. Best thing that I ever did. I can see all the sides of me now. I feel at peace.

My theory simplified? We all have different sides to our personalities. In a normal personality, the parts are mostly harmonious and healthy with some crazy areas. In a poorly functioning personality, only the percentages are different, and too much of the personality is unhealthy and conflicted. When a person is in denial about the parts, the problems are projected onto others and the relationship suffers.

We all have our unique temperament, parts of our parents' personalities and all the remnants of our childhood personalities. Traumas, early attachments and temperament all determine how harmonious the parts of us are. In therapy, I show my patients their different parts, and help them to resolve their internal conflicts. The therapeutic relationship over time becomes internalized. It acts as an internal soother and secure base.

Alla, you picked two interesting articles of mine to send to you. "Love: The Most Important Ingredient in Happiness" is a review of my Ph.D. dissertation from Psychology Today (Horn, 1976). In my research, "The Effects of Interpersonal and Economic Resources on the Quality of Life" (Gordon, 1975), I looked at the different resources that people can exchange (Foa, 1974). I found that love, power, information, money, goods, services, and sex all contributed to happiness, but love by far contributed the most to happiness.

Money is no doubt a factor. Poverty brings suffering that only money can cure. Now, here is the interesting part. The rules of money and love are opposite. For example, if you were poor as a child, but became rich as an adult, you would really appreciate the money.

The same is not true for love. If you did not get enough healthy love as a child, you become both needy and defensive. You may alternate between demanding love and unconsciously pushing it away. You don't seem to trust it. You don't seem to feel that it is enough. The difference is that we all need healthy love to develop a normal personality. If we don't get enough of it in childhood, it damages our personalities. No amount of current love can repair that childhood loss. No amount of overcompensation of ego, money, fame, etc., can fix the loss of a healthy parental relationship. That repair usually requires a long-term, emotionally corrective relationship, such as is found in psychotherapy.

After my dissertation, I went on to write, "Systems-Object Relations View of Marital Therapy: Revenge and Reraising" (Gordon, 1982). I wondered if love is so important to happiness, then why are we so poor at securing a lasting love? To better understand this problem I combined two theories: Systems theory and Object Relations theory. Systems theory states that every part of a system affects all the other parts. Every person in the family system exerts an influence on each other's behaviors. Our roles in our family helped to keep the family operating. We were a rescuer, scapegoat, messiah or all, depending on the needs of the family system. These roles eventually become part of our unconscious dramas that we take into other relationships.

If there was conflict in the family system outside of the child, then there will be conflict inside the child's personality system. The original family system—that is our parents' personalities, their marriage, how they treated us, and our temperament—becomes a large part of our unconscious personality.

Object Relations has to do with parts of our personality that are formed from our temperament and our perceptions of our primary love relationships. Our relationship with our caregivers became internalized in our unconscious and remains a core part of our personality. These internal objects act as automatic categories when we perceive others, fitting people into designated roles. Others become the object of our desires and fears based on our unconscious internalizations.

Psychoanalysts refer to it as "Object Relations" and not "Personal Relations" since we often see others so subjectively. How we see each other is based not only on the reality of the person but also based on our own personalities. The more disturbed the personality, the more others become objects of a person's projections. The object of desire can be a body part or article of clothing as with perversions or to a substance or drugs as in an addictive disorder.

The core of our personality is formed by our attachments in early childhood while the brain is still forming (Schore, 1994, 2003). We unconsciously try to repeat the patterns of attachment in our current love relations. Researchers looked at relationship patterns in 50 young adults who were studied 20 years earlier as infants. Overall, 72% of the adults had the same attachment behaviors (secure versus insecure) in their love relationships as they had as infants with their mothering figure (Walters, 2000). If there are childhood traumas with loss, aggression, neglect, impingement or exploitation, this drama becomes part of the self. This drama repeats itself in future attachments to achieve the same emotional result as in childhood. If there was conflict with a parent, so then there will be conflict with our current love. When we enter into intimacy, we regress and repeat our unconscious emotional past, without realizing it. Many feel that a new love (a new ideal parent) will magically break this drama.

Our unconscious does not perceive the new love as new, but rather in terms of our first loves. We can repeat the past by:

1. Picking someone with similar qualities of a parent. (Example: you find that you have the most passion for a lover who is as critical as your parent);

2. Unconsciously provoking the partner into acting like the parent figure. (Example: you provoke your lover's criticism by acting as a child); or

3. Distorting the perception of the partner to seem like the parent. (Example: you misperceive your partner as being unfairly critical.)

We do any or all of these—picking, provoking, and

distorting—in order to repeat unconsciously the imprinting and traumas (Gordon, 1998). In love, we return to the past, one way or another.

Must we be slaves to these patterns? No. Insight can disrupt self-defeating patterns. We can make a distinction when we are upset between how much of our feelings are coming from our own issues and how much are attributable to the other person. If we reflect on these insights rather than act out, our intimacies might not become the toxic waste dump for our past conflicts. Defensive people try not to think about the past or their patterns, but unconsciously act out the past in their relationships.

People often take out on their partner the unresolved anger and fears they had for a parent. With this revenging, they never detoxify the past, but only reinforce it. They don't learn and grow to love maturely.

Therapy can change these love dramas through an emotionally corrective relationship with the psychotherapist. It is intensive work.

I also believe that many of the therapeutic aspects of the emotionally corrective relationship in psychotherapy can be found in a healthy intimacy. I think that people can have emotional growth in marriage. It requires self-reflection. If there is denial, it's not possible. That is why I don't want a defensive partner...

What are your views on all of this? I am eager to learn more about you!

Warmly,
Robert.

Alla's request for these papers and our interpretations of them was an overture to the themes of our relationship...

Alla agreed that love is the most important ingredient in happiness. But she believed that a romantic hero would come and bring everlasting happiness to her. He would be the supplier of unconditional love and the fulfiller of her dreams. He would tolerate all her problems as a demonstration of his love. The article on revenge or re-raising is about achieving a mature love through sometimes-painful truth about one's self and one's childhood. Alla rejected this concept for the "just love me" cure.

I used this as an opportunity to share my feelings about the nature of happiness and a mature relationship. No one is entitled to a good relationship. Good looks, sexiness, charm, power or money can attract, but they are insufficient to maintain a good relationship. Relationships take work. If it requires too much hard work, something is wrong.

I warned Alla that if one does not understand one's troubled history and personality, any love would become subjugated to the past. I was asking Alla whether she knew the difference between infatuation and mature love.

Everyone has faults, but some faults are relationship killers, such as hostility and defensiveness.

Date: Sept. 29
From: Alla
To: Robert
Subject: My Rhapsody in Blue

Hello, Phantom of deep wisdom.
My Russian time 1.32 a.m. long day...
Do you wait for me?
You wrote: "What immortal hand or eye, dare frame an Alla?"
Thank you Robert! I serve and worship Blake.

So you want to see even more photos of me? Take everything.

(I do love to give!) Take this madness...take this wisdom, I think...they always wanted to belong to you.

(Alla expressed an instant intimacy that went beyond flirting. Alla seemed to feel that she and I were destined to be together. Already, Alla had hired me for the role of her idealized lover. Instant intimacy is about a projected fantasy, not discovery. It is a projection of one's wishes and dramas onto a suitable subject. I see all this now, but at the time I loved it.)

I know that I am nothing compared to you. Oh, yes. You surpass me in many ways. You are a Pro.

I am only a poor amateur with aristocratic manners...And I know that amateurs built the ark. Professionals built the Titanic. (Smiiilllleeee.) I am like you. I am not defensive. I do not want to be with someone who is defensive. I need to be understood.

(Just what I needed to hear. But defensive people don't know if they are defensive.)

Fasting for Yom Kippur is very spiritual. I need to re-read a thick scroll of Torah, to light candles, go to Synagogue...I'm dreaming to see Majestic Jerusalem...I mentally share this holiday with you. Le Chaim. Have a meaningful fast and meditation.

(So many Russian Jews converted and assimilated to survive. Alla reads the Torah, goes to synagogue and knows Hebrew. Maybe she is part Jewish.)

So you loved your psychoanalysis? It was the best thing you ever did?

I want be able to say: I have found my twin, my soul mate, my 5th Element. Best thing that I ever did.

(When I first read this, in my idealization of her, I distorted what she meant. I thought she also had an analysis. Only when I reread this did I see my distortion. Alla thought that finding her twin, her soul mate was a cure. She replaced cure by truth with cure by narcissistic

love. Her twin would be worthy of her love. Her projected ideal, not insight, would be her salvation.)

Did you see my telephone home number on my business card I sent, I just wonder?

(What would it be like to speak with her? A voice conveys so much information about personality.)

I am ready for global changes. Gosh! (Here better to use more dirty words!!) I am really tired to live here.

I wait for a worthy real offer, Robert. London, Paris... Allentown. (Smile)

(Alla was saying, "Robert, make me an offer, ask me to marry you." This instant chemistry was a projected idealized fantasy of the knight who will rescue her. When new lovers feel as if they have always known each other, it is recalling the original idealized love for a parent.

Children hope for the idealized parent to come back to them. Once a child begins to see the parent as inadequate, the child longs for the return of the earlier idealized parent. I wondered about her relationship with her parents. I wondered how much of her past she would share.)

I don't mind going anywhere as long as it's an interesting path. I have been down this road a few times, but this trip must be more pure!

(Alla stated that she has been down this road before, but she did not seem to understand why her relationships had failed. This was a big clue that she might go down that same road again—with the same results.)

I do not have a mission in Saint Petersburg anymore. (I am a superstar here—it's boring.) Maybe God wants me somewhere else...

It seems that you think that the past will determine love...

Do you want to know my opinion?

I cannot diagnose anything. (And you?) I just listen to my heart. Maybe, I need a marriage with smart, successful, rich Prince, for example? (Big grin) I'm tired of being alone. I am missing my other half. I need a good, strong man (best teacher and cute joker!) at my side...Oops...excuse me...I should stop this chaotic flow of consciousness....I know that people need to pay you to listen to their confessions...I think the real art of conversation is not only to say the right thing at the right time, but also to leave unsaid the wrong thing at the tempting moment. Am I right? (Smile)

Alla (you can hear my cute giggles...)

This seductive letter drew me deeper into her. Alla seemed narcissistic, but most children who had beauty and/or extraordinary talents and were greatly admired often develop some narcissism. Her narcissism did not seem to be at the level of a relationship toxin. Narcissists that are toxic exploit others and have little capacity for concern or remorse. Alla claimed to be modest, giving, and not defensive.

Alla responded to my article on personality and marriage with a hint of a rebuttal. She questioned my reliance on insight. This was a big hint that Alla disagreed with the need to look into the past. Rather, Alla felt that when messianic love came all would be right in her life. How much are her reactions cultural? There is no translation for the word "insight" in Russian. They have no words for it. The culture has been more supportive of magical solutions than psychological ones.

Ironically, I picked Alla partly because of her interest in psychology, but her interest was only a defense against it. It was her need to master intellectually the science that represented her worst fears. Rather Alla believed in fate, God's will, and her intuition. Alla believed that these forces determined the course of love. When destiny gave her a hero, then she would be content.

Every morning I rushed to my computer to receive Alla's e-mails and photos. I loved the gifts of her photos. I kept thinking of her, but at this point, I could see that it was an impractical relationship. I was ready to end my relationship with Alla.

I had enjoyed the flirting and I was very flattered by her

interest, but I was really worried about her maturity. I wrote to her that there were too many difficulties and differences between us and that sadly, it had to end.

Date: Sept. 29
From: Alla
To: Robert
Subject: I wait for Spring

Hello, Robert.

I think of old lovers, if we should meet would appear as ice statues to me now...I melt now that you are in my life...

(Poetic and flattering, but I have former lovers as friends. Why doesn't she? Do they end so badly? Will I eventually become an ice statue to her as well?)

You are probably already sleeping; I should leave you for now, but not before my comment for you...You told me that you are too old for me...Thank you for these mature words, my dear...I am 3000 years old...I was born not yesterday...(Warm smile)

You are the first man in my life who wants to be just my friend! (Laughs aloud)

When will you touch me, I just wonder?

Robert, I am thinking of you 24 hours per day. Sometimes, I think: 'Alla, you are mad!'

My thoughts are fixated on you. Gosh! I love your smile. I admire you for so many reasons. Your letters drive me crazy. I really enjoy conversing with you each and every day. (I know you only 3 days! Wild madness!) I want to know and to predict each movement of your soul. I want to activate your internal forces. I want to see you near and natural. I want to eat and drink your essence. May I?

(Now I regret my words to end it.)

So...Let's try to be friends...Be close to me...Do you want me to say: 'Robert, I shall not allow you to love anybody except me?' I insist that you should love me! (smile) I hope you can't resist...

You can read about my aristocratic roots in my last interview...Today I am sending to you this magazine with me on the cover page. It was just printed. Now, each passenger on the international flights has this magazine. If you arrive tomorrow to see me for a romantic supper, you would have the opportunity to receive your own copy of this magazine with my photo and frank scandalous details of my life. Rich material for psychological research! (Big grin)

How do I know about Judaism? Jews accompany me all my life. Many times I was the participant in Jewish political organizations. I was 20 when I received an invitation for a huge banquet in Moscow with the president of Israel. I even spoke "Shalom" to his wife. I know and I like this culture, Robert.

I love things, which were tested for 3000 years.

Almost 10 years ago, I listened to magnificent lecture about anti-Semitism. I have received the invitation for a meeting in the President-Palace in Moscow. I saw all the cream, all the magnificence of Russian-Jewish society, Robert.

My first love was a Jew, my professor. I was a virgin. I was younger than he by 22 years. Ha!

(Was I part of her drama of the father/teacher/lover? Perhaps she hoped to complete her unfinished business with her father through me.)

Don't think, that I am crazy! Please!

You have chosen the very strange woman on the Internet.

(She has reason for concern. I said from the start that I was looking for a well adjusted partner.)

I don't want to flirt with you.

I am a Woman. Though I can be like a child sometimes.

(All people have periodic regressions. But this qualification was a warning. People often use euphemisms for their mental problems. They

say, "It's just my temper." "It's just my nerves." "Just acting like a child."
It could be a sign of rationalizations to come.)

Ask God for the answer...Listen to your heart...I know
what I want and I will wait for your decision...

I thank God he led me to you. Anyway...

Please call me, Robert.

Welcome to my crazy world, dear.

I will be at home after 10 p.m. today (Russian time)

11 p.m., 12, 1 a.m. No problem.

I will wait for your voice.

Sleep well, Phantom of Destiny.

Alla

Alla effortlessly and smoothly seduced me towards her. She
was not about to be rejected. Alla was an effective siren.

I kept failing in my attempts to back out of this relationship.
I finally accepted her invitation to call.

The next day, Sunday afternoon, I called Alla. I felt more
anxious than I anticipated. Alla clearly excited me. I was
infatuated with her, but I was concerned about such distance and
differences. I wanted our conversation to be a disappointment
so I would be relieved of my conflict, but I also hoped it would
be great. This conflict only increased my infatuation. Dangerous
and forbidden romances heighten passion. This may be due to
the excitement of acting out of Oedipal wishes (Stoller, 1979).
Our first loves were forbidden fruits. We all retain the thrill of
wishing to do something naughty and rebellious. At the very
least the physiological state of arousal, be it erotic or fearful,
can temporarily enhance infatuation (Stephan, Berscheid and
Walster, 1971). People who met during a crisis, when they are

vulnerable or even on a roller coaster are more likely to become attracted to one another (Meston, 2003).

I remember when I first heard her voice. It surprised me. I was expecting a haughty, intellectualized voice and not her sweet charming one.

"Hello? Robert? How are you? I've waited 30 years to speak with you." Alla said with a feminine and playful intonation.

"Alla, you sound as lovely as you look, dam it! Your voice goes with your eyes."

"Thank you, you have a good taste for wild exotic things. Fortunately for you and me, I am even more fun in the flesh, my dear. I told you. I am a Taurus. I am the perfect child of Venus. I am created to give and take love."

"I believe you. Your English is very good."

"Much of it is by intuition. My intuition was right about you Robert. I've known you before in another life. I am sure of it."

"Uh, huh!" I said with a mocking tone.

"Uh, huh." Alla sang back. "Robert, Robert, why YOU?"

"I know it's not practical."

"Not my favorite word. By the way, you are a very sensual and sexual person. Gosh! I mean you are a spicy, hot and crazy, passionate pirate! It's impossible! My intuition knew this!"

"This makes matters worse."

"Oh, Robert, what will become of this madness? Isn't it too rare to throw away?"

I was high after we spoke. I could not remember ever having such a flirtatious, playful first conversation. I felt more drawn to her. I felt the situation getting out of hand. Now what?

Chapter 4

You Can't Be Intimate with a False Self

Karen came into the session looking exhausted since she brought conflict to everything she did. She had an ability to make simple tasks difficult.

"I'm too tired for this. What can I talk about? Oh yeh, I went shopping with my mom. We went to Neiman Marcus. It was such a good sale...In Sephora I got this really, really great makeup...We found this place for lunch...my mom loves pepperoni pizza with the thick crust. I saw these Donna Karan pants for my mom. She's an eight. I wanted to buy them for her. She couldn't decide. She said, 'It's beautiful, but where would I wear them?' We had such a great time. I was actually feeling OK, until I realized I had to see you."

Karen talked on the surface of her existence. It deadened the listener. When people speak to relate and convey meaning, there can be intimacy (Langs, 1983). There is no intimacy when a person speaks to just dump or speaks to obscure meaning. When someone does that, you feel like you are being used as the other person's audience or toxic waste dump. They don't want to look at their stuff. They just want to leave it with you, walk away, and feel a bit relieved. Worse than that is actual obscuring meaning or lying. These people avoid or distort the truth and construct a reality to fit the drama of their imagined lives. They use language to hide, manipulate and exploit. Karen dumps and obscures. It is part of her defense. She doesn't relate to me. She keeps me on the other side of her verbal smoke screen. After giving nothing of herself she expects something in return.

Karen expects me to find meaning in the shallow content of her false self. This false self was created for the outside world. Her false self is used to protect her true self from further harm (Winnicott, 1960). You can't be intimate with a false self. She dumps her stories like a load of laundry. She has no interest in wondering about the stains. A therapist must listen carefully. But a therapist doesn't have to attend to every word during periods of dumping and obscuring. A good therapist knows when to jump in like a mother who hears a dangerous silence or a different quality to a cry.

In psychotherapy, a person can learn to relate more meaningfully when the therapist interprets what is not said, but what is felt and meant. At which point the patient must make a decision, to be defensive or to learn to relate more constructively. At this point I am not sure if Karen is only defensive or incapable of meaningful communication.

Suddenly Karen asked, "I think he's wrong. What do you think?"

I had to come out of my protective numbed state to piece together the last fragments of meaningful phrases from Karen's heap of words. Karen was dumping and externalizing blame with no insight. I had no idea what to say about her complaints about her new boyfriend. Karen wanted me to support her perceptions. She wanted me to "validate" her. I dislike that pop-psych concept. How would I know if what she was telling me was true? If I agreed with distorted perceptions I would reinforce her problems. If I disagreed with her too early, she would feel attacked.

I clarified, "Karen, I know that you are upset, but I'll have a better idea how you see people by your transferred perceptions on to me..."

"I perceive you fine. Ed is a typical man. He thinks he's always right. Most men are like that. So are you."

Karen didn't want to hear what I had to say because that would disrupt her need of me as a passive audience. Karen feared what I might say so she kept talking. When she asked, "What do you think?" she was just checking to see if I was still receiving her dumping. I was to remain her dumping ground, occasionally agree, or remain silent. For now, I must be her container. After a while more meaningful material might bubble up. And abruptly it did.

"My father molested me. I don't miss him. My mother is my best friend. She never remarried so I could have a good childhood. She suffered a lot in her life. I really admire her strength. I wish I were more like her. I know I have problems with men because of my father."

She first spoke of this when I treated her briefly four years ago, but it never went anywhere. How could I help her with men, if she refused to talk about this trauma? What most people do not realize is that most of the time in psychotherapy is wasted by the patient resisting the treatment. The more patients unconsciously needs their symptoms, the more the resistance to treatment. Karen's existential job in life was to be a victim. She might complain, but she was not about to be jobless.

The body protects itself with resistance against foreign influence. It fights off viruses and toxic bacteria as invaders against the body. Personality in the same manner protects itself from the invasion of others. When a parent traumatizes a child, the child forms an extra strong protective resistance. What surprises new therapists the most is when a patient comes into treatment complaining of symptoms and then spends most of the time resisting change for the better. In psychoanalytic psychotherapy, analyzing the resistance and defenses is more important than focusing on the symptoms. This is because we analysts assume that most people would over time learn from life if it weren't for their resistance to change and defensiveness to critical feedback.

I work hard helping patients learn to resist toxic people and their own toxic thoughts. I help them test reality to see what thoughts and what people are safe, good, and nurturing and which are not. The deeper the trauma, the more indiscriminate are the resistance and stronger are the defenses. If a patient's resistance to change and defensiveness are too strong, there is little hope for improvement. They have a psychological autoimmunity disorder. They attack themselves and constructive people as if they were enemies. To Karen I was a virus.

Karen was also a mystery. In college Karen was home sick. She had a suicide attempt when her boyfriend rejected her. Why did Karen have difficulty separating and have abandonment issues? Sex abuse may make these symptoms worse, but they generally start from attachment problems.

If Karen thought that telling me that her mother was a size eight would help her to find a lasting love, we had a lot of work to do. A therapist should ask a patient a question if it is to deepen the reflective process. Finally towards the end of the session, I asked,

"Karen I remember you telling me that your problems with men are because of your father molesting you."

"Sure. Sure."

"How old were you?"

"I think I was six. But I've been over this many times in therapy. There is no need to dwell on it. I need help with my life now."

Karen went on to another topic.

The age of a trauma affects the developmental arrest. By six, most children have already mastered separation from mother and formed much of their basic personality. Karen's hostility towards men made sense because of the father. But separation issues are usually related to traumas before age six, within the first two to three years of life (Mahler, 1974). They have to do with the mothering figure's interaction with the child's temperament. Some of Karen's symptoms didn't fit with psychological research.

At the end of the session I had Karen take the Minnesota Multiphasic Personality Inventory (MMPI-2) in the waiting room. It is the most scientific and most used objective psychological test of personality problems in the world. I give it to most my patients. I have used it to study changes in personality traits over years of treatment. I told Karen that we could review her scores in her next session.

Karen said, "You didn't give me this test last time,"

"I didn't think you would stay long."

"What makes you think I will this time?"

Chapter 5

Early Warning Signs

Alla's e-mails were usually several pages long, and came about twice a day. I generally only had time to make quick responses within her letters before I rushed off to work. For easier reading, I will relate most of the emails (and instant messages) as conversations.

Sept. 30

"Alla, I'm not sure I can make a romantic dinner with you tomorrow or anytime realistically. "

"Robert come to me. You and I could meet in Moscow...It is a huge mad city...Moscow is an anthill of running people. More than 10 million around you simultaneously! O-lala...Craziness. It's a rhythm of life as in New York City, but with another mentality...Moscow is our Jerusalem with huge distances, expensive restaurants, and crowds of tourists; if you want to see big Russian disorder—come to Moscow...I don't love this city. I wouldn't live there. I've had many opportunities to remain there forever, but I always came back to my hometown...

You already know, I prefer a European atmosphere with pleasant whispers of English, French, Italian, or German in my ear all the time. But if you never been in Russia maybe, it is a good choice for you..."

"Alla, if I would go to Russia, it wouldn't be to sightsee. It would be to see you."

"Really? Then it is a better choice to fly directly to Saint Petersburg.

It's not a secret, everyone knows of this, the MOST beautiful women of Russia live here. You will have a unique opportunity to see the proof of this fact...I promise to show you the most attractive and clever girls. I am not worried though...I can capture your libido, my precious friend. It is easy! I would be glad to be your guide; if you will want...I know each stone and street in my hometown, one of the most beautiful cities in the world...I can show for you the best, VIP places. I am queen here...

You'll see my T.V. fashion show, my articles in magazines, my paintings, my designs, and bla-bla-bla...+ 1000 photos...

Saint Petersburg is a friendlier, more cultured atmosphere than Moscow. Certainly, you will receive an invitation to visit my modest home; the special place for only privileged tourists...I think it will be an intriguing study for you of this strange Russian UFO with the name of Alla. I think, any personality will be best observed in her natural environment...Am I right?"

"Alla what will become of this late summer's night dream?"

"The best way to break this late summer's night dream is to meet. Puck corrects mistakes in the end. Oh, why YOU Robert?"

"And why You? You are so wonderful and so out of range."

"Robert, I really wish there could be insurance for the kaput heart. If I will fall in love with you, it's not an Apocalypse anyway. I am willing to see where this may lead us..."

"Falling in love is a temporary delusional state."

"I assert that your 5-year analysis will not be enough. I think for the goal to study me, it is necessary about 50 years...I am like a chameleon...I am the Milky Way...I am always new, endlessly...Though, I suppose, your professionalism will have the ability to break open all confidential codes of my soul within the next decades...On my Bible's oath, I've done a many mad things...I am a flame under ice...I bet, you think I am crazy... You need a silent, good, simple woman, without a bullet in her head; am I right?"

(She was right. I did not want a woman with a bullet in her head. Alla was an exciting woman. However, was she someone who would

make a mature partner? Alla saw the world in terms of the extremes. This is called "splitting", as in splitting reality into black or white. The choice for her was either a wild personality or a "silent, good, simple" personality. She must act out her drama or feel empty inside.)

"Alla, how about someone exciting and easy to be with? I loved the pictures you sent. Thanks."

"You wish more pictures of me?.. I have a lot of photos from my modeling...My Lord! I don't know what kind of photos you want to see; Alla as superstar, Alla as natural child, Alla as artist-designer who has a perfect reputation and earned the respect of the most influential people of this city...My reputation almost is sacred in this city...as sexy Siren or Cold Queen or Alla as model, cover girl bird known by her plumage?"

What a charming siren. I knew I was in deep trouble. I kept becoming more and more infatuated with this fascinating woman. Yet, I also wanted to get out of it. She seemed both wonderful and strange.

Alla often wondered, "WHY YOU?" Any man could fall in love with Alla. I was later to learn the deeper meaning of this phrase. Alla had offers of marriage from many rich, handsome men. Alla was clearly confused and conflicted about being in love with a much older man who was not a rich, European Adonis. Why me? Perhaps I represented the ideal parent who would make her feel unconditionally loved and secure. Reason told me that this had to end. My passion told me that I must meet this beautiful, fascinating woman.

Oct. 1

"Hello my 5th Element. I repeat your name as a Mantra. I finally found you...You can be a lousy therapist to yourself right now. I want to be your psychologist...sole hope...strong link...rebirth...full-blooded shout...tears of happiness, warm madness...I can be Sun for you...We have a stock in eternity...I do not want to be only a temptation...I am worth more, much more, my dear."

"Alla, because this relationship is impossible—it makes it so romantic. It is safe from passion-robbing realities. But the realities are against this going further. You can have your pick of wonderful men that would fit your life. I want to settle down into a marriage, and what would our marriage look like in 10 years? Think about it. You are an incredible woman. I never thought I would meet someone like you. I wish that you would find your knight who is worthy of all your passion. But our relationship is just not practical."

Chapter 6

Idealization and Devaluation

Extroverted, seductive but distrustful of closeness....
problems with intimacy...anxiety and depression
from possible childhood trauma...This patient is very
defensive...look for idealization and devaluation and denial...
Not a good candidate for insight psychotherapy...consider
cognitive-behavior therapy or supportive therapy for some
symptom relief and medication for anxiety and depression..."

The MMPI-2 confirmed that Karen was afraid of looking
at herself. Her scores indicated that her anxiety and depression
were not just because of her current state of loneliness, but
probably from childhood traumas. There is a strong relationship
between losses and traumas with parents in childhood and later
major depression in adulthood (Bemporad and Romano, 1993;
Browne, 1995).

Karen didn't ask about her MMPI-2 results and I didn't
bring it up. I had told her that I would have the results ready for
this session. She didn't want to know the results. She was too
defensive. I waited for the right time.

Karen's unconscious compromise between her need for
love and her fear of it was to move in and out of relationships,
over and over again. She lived for the magic of infatuation, then
became disappointed, and looked for another infatuation. She
also felt dependent but feared dependency. This pattern of in
and out object relations will express itself with me. Luepnitz
(2002) stated that a goal of the talking cure is, "To choose

solitude freely, to love and engage fully..." Karen was unable to choose. She reacted to others according to her fears and defenses.

"You are supposed to be the best. Why aren't you helping me?" Karen complained.

Karen acted haughty as a defense against her feelings of worthlessness. Karen overcompensated by believing that she had to have the best of everything, since she felt deep inside that she was damaged goods. I was another best charm for the moment.

Karen idealized me as her guru and believed that I had the magic answers. Underneath idealization is its opposite, devaluation. As soon as I was unable to provide her with magic, I was devalued and verbally stoned as a false prophet. She did the same in her love relationships. When she fell in love she over idealized her lover. When her lover could not meet her impossible expectations, she devalued him.

The splitting of her perception of others in terms of all good or all bad reflected her fragmented self. She projected her grandiose self or her damaged self on to others (Kohut, 1966, 1971; Kohut, Goldberg, & Stepansky, 1984).

Karen said, "How are you able to get these fees for what you do?"

"How are you able to keep a good guy with your devaluing?"

"Is putting me down supposed to be good for my self-esteem?"

I said, "Good self-esteem comes from acknowledging faults and all the sides of you. Constructive criticism will help you to develop a more secure identity."

"Sure. Sure. I don't feel better, I feel worse from your therapy, Dr. Gordon."

I clarified, "You brought your anger and distrust into our relationship. Instead of wondering where it came from, you blame your current relationship. If you have the courage to see this pattern, you might begin to break it." My voice conveyed concern and warmth, despite Karen's aggression. I was able to contain and make sense of her devaluation of me.

Patients often see me as the worst parts of themselves (projection), and the worst parts of their care givers (transference). I often have to clarify who I am. Once the reality of me is clarified, then I might make an interpretation of why a patient is distorting me. Once patients begin to recognize the disowned and projected parts of them, or transferred feelings about their parents, they will distort less in their relationships.

"Now I don't have enough courage? You blame me for everything. You are provoking me. Is this part of the therapy?"

Karen needed to fight with me. She would rather fight with me than look at herself.

I clarified, "No I cannot provoke you. If I were the main cause of your reactions, then how could I interpret what is unconsciously coming from you? Your degree of aggression cannot be explained by the here and now reality. You carry a lot of unconscious hostility that is waiting for a justification to come out."

Karen said, "I don't have anything unconscious. I would know!"

Much of personality is unconscious, particularly conflicts (Geraskov, 1994). We have parts of our parents' personalities, our attachment history, our childhood emotions and experiences all stored in our implicit memory. We have an unconscious affecting us in ways that most people never imagine. From earliest childhood, we store unfinished emotional business into our unconscious, but it is not a passive warehouse. It is affecting our moods, perceptions and motives. When we fall in love, our unconscious enacts its love drama with a predictable pattern. What was in Karen's unconscious? I wondered if it was possible to go there. The cost of her not resolving her conflicts was to be without a stable love relationship. But could she tolerate what she might find within herself? Most people avoid insight and suffer. This might be Karen's fate.

Chapter 7

Explosion Number One

Date: Oct. 5
From: Alla
To: Robert
Subject: Bad dream about you

Hello, stranger...

Well...well...well...You have the conclusion of your long meditation...So, as far as I understand, we never meet, my sweet friend...

Am I right?

I can't have a long, wise comment for you, because I am in the Internet cafe in Frankfurt and haven't a lot of time for it and I am tired from the show.

BUT I feel, you need a few ideas from me. Right Now!

Robert, I feel upset...I must admit.

It looks like a bad dream about you.

Becuase...(I am sorry for my spelling, fucking German keyboard!!!),

You have disorder in your brain.

You're in a trap of your illusion!

I am just trying to erase the bullshit from your wise head.

(Alla's temper, grandiosity, inner emptiness, and flipping between idealization and devaluation of me is so clear in this email.)

You don't want to risk a life with me.
I understand after reading your mad letter.
I am ready to go away from you.

Am I right, my fallen Angel?

You can't imagine, how upset I am, that you said such fucking bullshit to me.
I am not your guru.
Do you really want to know?

I need the usual things for life.
De facto, deeply inside me, I want the human things—a warm house...green flowerbed under the windows...Burning candles...Tasty supper...Rest and coziness...Love, protection, and care...I simply want to fall asleep on his strong shoulder and to not worry about tomorrow's day.

I need to settle down with my 5th Element.

What else?...I want to become his strong, safe fortress, sweet rest, gentle pleasure, and eternal inspiration...Be his prayer and hope, his unearthly love, his alpha, beta and omega... not simply a wife.

I want to become close to him and be simply happy...I dream to find the partner of my life, a teacher, and best friend, have fun with him, to find this feeling to be finally at home. My Lord, Pls, show me the place!

I have a small saga for you before I leave...

I have been trying to find my soul mate all my 30 years... I know about global loneliness...I know about fathomless, soundless loneliness, ruthless, unrestrained, ice, cheerless loneliness, vain, unbearable, helpless, and infinite loneliness, groundless and sleepless loneliness...immeasurable...When it seems, that (on the one hand) all world belongs to you, each point of your body contains continents, oceans, flora and fauna, clouds, wind, fire, sun...It seems, you can even fly and go for a walk on clouds...

And on the other hand you belong...to nobody...And all this grandiose volume inside you...is simply boundless and empty...And you fall...you fall...you are falling in this huge black hole...and your skin absorbs even this black...black...night without stars...Then you feel that your internal beauty and perfect harmony begins slowly...very slowly to die and wither, as a broken flower...you cling to air...cold fingers onto emptiness, a lot of wine only increases the sound of a suppressed shout...a suffocating vacuum embalms your heart...And words 'all will be good'—do not work any more. And the brain does not analyze. And, you think, God does not exist...and there is NO satisfaction...Ice-covered bed...And you moan, you mentally shout, 'Fuck! Where are you? Where are you, my love, my hope, and my soul mate! Pls, appear. Please, I am almost half-dead and I waiting for you for SO long...long time...ALL my life...' But...Nobody is to answer...and you only hear the rhythm of your heart.

You are Solo in absolute silence...Eternal search without a long-awaited result...And the muses sleep...Only blunt, unearthly pain deep inside...And you think if you will not give back this pain to somebody...that the next minutes you can become blind from tears...you can be drowned in tears...And the pain again will penetrate in you deeper and deeper...As one hundred poisonous stings in my throat...and it seems that my heart will dry up from an imaginary bleeding...And you are ready to give to somebody all your money, all your riches for an opportunity to simply fall asleep...rigid, sharp, malicious Despair...or self-destruction?

(Alla was describing her mood swings that could be from a Bi-Polar disorder, and/or Borderline Personality Structure. "...unearthly pain deep inside...and you think if you will not give back this pain to somebody..." *This is an example of projective identification. It is a primitive way to get rid of bad feelings by giving them to someone else. It is a way to make someone you depend on to feel as bad as you feel. Alla's grandiosity was an over compensation of her fragile self-esteem. Rejection was too painful for her.*

In order to keep her pain from becoming unbearable, Alla gave the pain to another. A person with a Borderline Personality Structure often provokes the partner into similar feelings. The person is relieved once he or she has caused pain and suffering of the partner. Projective identification helps relieve tension within the person, but it destroys relationships.)

You said that you need to settle down.
Do I understand?
Really, do I seem so stupid???
Be sure. I DO understand.
What would a marriage of us look like in 10 years?
Ok...I will answer. (Fuck! I am losing my time at this internet café)! I must to stop. Oh, help!
How I can to help you, my Angel? How?

Look at My Spiritual Path To Higher Creativity—
Ah, Robert. I studied about morphology, cosmology, genetic memory, platonic love, non-linear world. Feeling is the doorway to the world. I can in detail describe functions and structure of all 7 basic Chakras, structure of the Human Aura, Dao, Tarot, Chinese traditions based on the Book of Changes and the Kabalistic number symbolism...etc...I had read Castaneda, Krishnamurti, Osho, I know the doctrine Yoga (for example, Hatha Yoga, Suatmarama, Hypnosis...), I know of concept Samadhi or Shakti, I know about Energy-channels and resettlement of the soul.

(Alla used magical thinking rather than insight for answers. I

chose to see Alla's magical thinking as a cultural, artistic, and spiritual distinction. I saw her thinking as metaphorical; she was a poet and very passionate. I chose not to see her as delusional.)

My old-warm-soul! You think I can plan a stupid, mad life for next 10 years, when I know—how relative 'TIME' is in the context of eternity?

Think about it!

Robert! I knew other ROBERT in my life.

Really my intuition was so STUPID??? Tell me, pls.

Gosh! You are in a trap of your illusion! Help! Help, people!

I don't care about time and distances. I don't care about correct, practical, and fucking convenient decisions. I need much more.

I like revolt and chaos more than fatal order. I don't care about the opinions of common people.

(Although Alla stated that she wanted a marriage, she was unable to say that she could commit to a relationship. People with internal chaos feel anxious with normalcy. They devalue it as boring out of envy. They often cause chaos in the relationship so that their internal world fits the external relationship.)

You said—We met in cyberspace.

We met many times before, my friend. Are you kidding?

I've appeared many times in your dreams. I was a star, warm wind, beacon...I was a shout of birds to help you to find me.

I have taken this body, these magic eyes, and this Jewish soul that you should find me among 1000 women!

10 years? Such Fucking bullshit! (That makes me insane!)

What are you talking about, Robert???????

As far as I remember, in a previous life, you were the sort of person who can to sell your soul to Devil, if you wanted someone or something.

What's happened? (Big grin)

I will follow your ideas. I will disappear, as you wish.

God prepared me as a rare and ancient wine.

Only for this unique purpose—do you want to know more about it?

I wanted to meet you face-to-face, seeing (and touching) will only tell if there is more than mental affection—But you are in a trap of your fears...I regret. I can't help you, if you can't to allow me to explore more.

I felt...that we were lovers many times before...I already knew it, when I first saw your smile in the photo you sent. I thanked God he led me to you...You were my best lover in my previous life. And many times before...It looked like a mad dance (animal and raw)...I think I saw your lazy exhaustion...Robert, I know a lot of things about you...I will tell you about it...in the next life...(Smile)

(Since Alla had no real concept of mature love, she defined love in terms of ideal romance and sexual satisfaction.)

God bless you, my friend...

I wish you happiness and REAL LOVE.

I gotta go...I want to be drunk...I need to forget about you.

Today I will dance a dirty Salsa, I suppose...

I'll try to think, that I just saw a bad dream...just bad dream...

You are just stranger in cyberspace...and yet I'm to deny that your name stays with me 24 hours a day, and it's not your photo in my bag in this minute. It's just fucking cyberspace.

There is only one chance for one life. And you will lose your chance to be with me.

So...................

See you in the next life, my hero.

In the next life, we will read Blake to each other with Gershwin playing softly. We will plan our sailing trips, and you will proudly tell everyone that I am your wife...

Are you ready?

I will disappear...
Are you sure???

(Do you wanna be drunk with me?)

Warm hugs
Phantom of Alla

Whenever Alla was upset her letters became very long, rambling, and her English broke down. This letter was much longer, and it required more than the usual editing for this book.

Alla felt that if I rejected her, it could only be because I was insane, and not due to any problem with her. Will this letter contain most of the issues to come?

Alla's reaction showed the symptoms of a Borderline Personality. Borderline Personality comes from the concept of a personality structure that is on the borderline between neurosis and psychosis. This is bad news for a healthy relationship.

A person with a Borderline Personality favors primitive defenses such as denial, projection, projective identification and splitting. The Borderline Personality has poor affect regulation. They have intense mood changes that define the partner in terms of the mood and not the reality of the person. The mood swings rewrite the relationship history and destiny. When in a high mood, the individual denies that anything can be wrong. When depressed or in a rage, the individual does not remember anything good. The idealization and devaluation of the partner is based on the person's emotions. The individual's self-concept and concept of the partner goes to extremes. The Borderline lives on an emotional roller coaster with the partner pulled along. All of these thoughts exist in my mind for an anxious split-second and are then repressed in deference to infatuation.

I saw these warning signs. I did not deny them. But I pushed aside this awareness, because Alla fascinated me. At some internal level, my knowledge of Alla's emotional problems remained as an anxiety for me. A mature love is a calm love. This was becoming an anxious love.

I focused on her wish to settle down to a normal relationship. Her need to impress me with her intellect and beauty had fallen away, yielding to a passionate plea for a loving home life. I accepted her problems as a small price to pay to be with such an amazing woman.

I became a psychologist partly because of my nurturing personality. There is a part of me than needs to care for others. Alla longed for a parent figure to care for her. We complemented each other, which helps to fuel the passion (Winch, 1958).

There is a degree of fear with intimacy. The fear is greatest when our first loves hurt us. When a person's first intimacy with a parent was injurious, then it's easier to fall in love when the unconscious knows it will not last. There is more need for defenses and walls when the possibility of committed love threatens. However, when a time bomb is ticking, why bother with the usual defenses? Although Alla feared love, my distancing and ambivalence made it safer for her to feel passion and pursue me. Conversely, my moving toward her increased her anxiety about commitment once more.

It was an intensely passionate love. This is the most dangerous kind because it is wedded to the most primitive side of personality. This sort of love is sexualized with a great deal of aggression at the core. Without maturity, the aggression blows up the relationship. Mature love does not need drama for its fuel.

Chapter 8

A Victim of Lost Love

I can't help you with men unless you talk about your father."

"I don't agree." Karen snapped.

"The price you pay for not dealing with the past is that it gets repeated in your relationships."

"Sure. Sure."

I said, "Children are naturally sexual and need non-seductive and non shaming parents so they can develop normally. Sex abuse can produce guilt, inhibitions, self-rejection, distrust..."

"Marsha, my therapist then told me that he must have been a psychopath. She said that I don't remember the sex abuse because it is a repressed memory."

"You don't remember a thing?"

Karen said, "No. That is typical of sex abuse."

Was this a matter of repression or was Karen made to believe that something happened when in fact there was no abuse? There is a false memory verses repressed memory debate in psychology. On the false memory side, research shows that children can have false memories implanted in them by experimenters (Loftus and Hoffman, 1989). Children are easily influenced to believe things. They are very suggestible. The child's suggestibility and tendency to confuse feelings with reality can create false memories. There are tragic cases where people have been sentenced to jail because children have falsely accused them of abuse. The Salem witch trials are reenacted again and again in many child abuse allegations (Gardner, 1987).

But much of the research shows that painful memories can be repressed and later remembered (Brown, 1999). I have found this in my work with patients. The mind avoids going to painful places. But repressed memories often come into awareness when therapy provides safety and empathy.

I have seen children who were abused and afraid to talk about it. Or when they did speak of it, the trauma of not being believed by the very people the child looked to for protection. I have also seen children brain-washed by a parent to believe that they were abused when they were not, and how that damages their ability to love later in life (Gordon, 1998, 2002). There is no black or white. Both possibilities can be true, false memories and repressed memories.

Memory is not a passive objective file of facts or a mechanical recording. It is part of an organic brain. It is affected by emotions and it is constantly being revised. Memory is fluid. I don't really know what happened in a person's past. Marsha, Karen's former therapist thought she knew. But I take nothing at face value. I look at many factors such as plausibility, consistency, and whenever possible corroborating witnesses. Many times a memory is a metaphor for a person's emotional history.

I began to work on a reconstruction of her emotional history. I was very careful not to assume too much since childhood memories can be any combination of fantasies and actual events (Arlow, 1991).

"What do you remember Karen?"

"I was six. He molested me. My parents separated over it. I never saw him again."

I questioned, "How does it feel to talk about it?"

"I feel nothing. And I don't dwell on it. My mother told me, 'Some things are the worst for the dwelling.'"

I clarified, "In therapy you can dwell constructively to help solve problems."

"I hate falling in love. But I feel empty without it."

Karen changed the topic, but not the theme. She was still talking about childhood trauma and her fear of closeness. Karen felt empty of a true self. Without a solid identity she feared losing herself to another. Her dependency needs brought her into the intimacy and her fear of losing her autonomy made her distance. She was caught in an "in and out program" in her love relations (Guntrip, 1969). She recreated love dramas to fill the void. Her drama was a repetition of a victim of lost love.

Chapter 9

Deciding to Fall in Love

Bob, come up. I'll be in the Poconos this weekend. I'll look over the emails and tell you what I think of your conflict then." Gerd Fenchel is a training psychoanalyst and the Dean of the Washington Square Institute in New York. Whenever he and his wife can, they often spend the weekends in their home in the Pocono Mountains. Gerd has a well-trimmed white beard and he looks more like Sigmund Freud every year. I drove about forty-five minutes north of Allentown to see my friend.

"Gerd, do we all regress when we fall in love?"

"Temporary regression, yes, but then the couple must deal with the real relationship in the real world. There are people who are completely overcome and consumed and lose their bearing."

"So it's normal to regress as long as there is enough reality in the madness?"

"Disturbed people escape their harsh existence and depression for the ecstasy found in intense love."

"Like the passion of Borderlines?" I asked.

"They have a primitive form of love and use sexuality and aggression to control others. They have magical expectations, want instant intimacy and have a constant need to be adored. With rejection or abandonment the rage comes out. They wish for an all-loving mother who understands them without words.

They go for mystical and magical solutions. Sadomasochism is not just the spice of passion as in a normal romance, but dominates those relationships. Passionate yes, but they are controlled by their emotional extremes and eventually their aggression destroys their relationships,"(Fenchel, 1998;2005).

After dinner, I showed him the e-mails from Alla. "Gerd, I am obsessed with Alla, but I am worried about her stability."

Gerd laughed, "You always bring me such entertaining conflicts. Alla is gifted and brilliant. You need that."

"Do you think that she is crazy?"

"I don't know. You dated one Russian before this and already you are an expert? Alla is dramatic, in other words a Russian."

"I'm not sure if she is disturbed or it's cultural."

"Bob, Russians had a hard life. They can be narcissistic and defensive. It's part of the culture. Religion was outlawed for 70 years. Spiritualism and superstition gave them comfort. They had no psychology to speak of until recently. It is hard to know how she really is. It might not be a personality disorder. You may be hearing her personal and cultural trauma. If that is all it is, after some time with you she might settle down. Maybe she sees that hope with you."

"I just ended it. I thought she was too wild. Then she broke down and told me how much she wanted a normal life."

"You need her wildness and she needs your order. But the same thing that excites you both now may later become intolerable. Yet, she may respond well to you. Some couples are able to keep the right balance of aggression and regard for one another that keeps the passion alive without the aggression destroying the relationship. You won't know how disturbed she is until you see all the sides of her in different circumstances; not just in letters and on the phone."

I handed Gerd several of her pictures.

"Oh my, are you sure this is really her? There are women who post pictures of models and get men to send them money."

"It's her. She sent me about thirty pictures. Most are from modeling over the last ten years, and some with her family, from her childhood and recently with her friends and on TV. She has a weekly fashion feature on TV in Saint Petersburg. She is a celebrity there."

"She's famous, has a Ph.D., looks like this and she wants you? OK, she is crazy. But she's too intriguing not to meet."

Oct. 7

"Alla, I had a long talk with a wise analyst friend. I needed some time and thought. I do want to explore this rare gift. You showed me an intimate side of you and you touched me with your feelings. "

"Hello, my dear Robert. It is actually difficult to start speaking to you now. I lose my internal balance when I speak with you. Something occurs inside me that I cannot supervise. You can make me very nervous and excited."

"I'm in the same condition."

"Thanks for allowing me to criticize you Robert."

"You were more intimate. So you want to settle down to a normal marriage?"

"Oh Robert it is impossible to speak about love and marriage before a personal meeting. It's cyberspace. Be cautious. For 100% trust nobody."

"Yes. I forbid you to speak of it."

"You will feel a difference in our cultures. You can't imagine how Russian mentality differs from your culture. Take more time for your conclusions, my dear. Robert, I know you much more than you can imagine. I am telling to you only 5% from my deep ideas. And English is not my native language...It is a new language for me...You receive little of my subtlety of thoughts and words!"

"Alla, do you have any idea how much I have fallen in love with you?"

"No, I don't know how much you love me! And when I do not see your new email more than after 24 hours per day or hear your voice—it seems that you do not exist...You keep telling me how much you want a sweet woman by your side...Do you really think, that I am such a cold Lady? Honey! I don't want to tease you. I don't want to play with you, flirt with you. If I'd want, you'd feel an erection 25 hours per day."

"I love how you tell time."

"If I'd want, I could show you my Real Sweetness...Oh, Gosh, I better don't talk about it."

"Please do."

"I know the boundless force of my charms! Do you understand?...Really...your professional intuition does not see it?"

"Alla, I'm not getting any work done on my paper and it is your fault!"

"I am really sorry! I know I have the charms to stop and destroy all work, my dear...And consequently I do not show you the huge stock of my tenderness..."

"Such consideration."

"I don't want to seduce you...Robert, I can be an Angel with a Devil's smile and Devil with an Angel's smile...My dear, do you understand my metaphors?...When we will make love, we shall connect body and spirit. You will tremble and shake from the soles of your feet to each cell deep inside your body... And when you will rest with me with your arm and leg over my body, you will then know that I am that UFO you found on the Internet...that this crazy Lady has been sent to you for a special purpose...I can keep you sexually young...I can be everything for you and much more."

"Sounds good my love; I can use a woman who is more than everything."

"Mentally now I touch your every tender spots, hair, shoulders, all over and you will feel fingers like petals...I would sing a sweet lullaby for you and as I stroke and caress your hair, while you will feel a deep calmness like warm, soft clouds around you...I can make so that you will be immersed in magic, sweet, air, blue Nirvana...I will be an island of tenderness...I'll embalm your body with my touches to your skin. I shall create you anew...You will think that you have appeared in this world the first time, that you did not know before feeling of love or happiness that you have no memory of previous experiences or disappointments in your life...Are you ready?.."

"Yes."

"Do you want be my best partner for this fantastic slow dance, Dr. Robert Gordon? Do you want to dance with me tonight, my favorite spirit?"

"Yes."

"I would want to hear you whisper: 'Alla, ALLA, I shall drink of you until I am close to death...And I shall want to die deep inside you, locked in a lover's embrace, my sucking on your tongue, kissing neck and breast...I do not fear your beauty, age, I bathe in it. Take me...We shall be together. I am totally fucked up...Alla, nothing is like this. Nothing...Nothing'..."

"A worthy way to die, when I am 80...not a minute before. We can practice for that final grand mort in the mean time. OK?"

"Yes my Swan..."

"You say that you don't want to seduce me? I love the way you don't seduce me. Please continue."

"Oh, Robert, I'd want to say for you many crazy things but my wisdom makes me silent."

"Where did this wisdom suddenly come from?"

"Do you sense my SWEETNESS?"

"That's not what I meant by 'sweetness' but I will not quarrel about your definition. Perhaps it's a cultural difference I could grow to love."

"I know the force of my charm. It is better if I do not show too much of this at this time. Words are empty, actions speak volumes. I am an action woman."

"I can handle your charm. Tell me more about your actions. I bet that you hate when I'm rational and practical."

"Fucking bullshit! I love your rational and practical ways. I really love your noble style...But, I must admit, sometimes you sound like a child, Robert! Leave cyberspace. It deforms reality. I'm MORE rational and practical than YOU. I can prove it to you."

"Really?"

"I have been solo for a long time. If anybody should be skeptical, it should be me...But I am not, I believe in Love and God...I am willing to PROVE my love to you....Listen to your heart, not your psychology. Shit!—Do not predict."

"You are right."

"Unfortunately. I am right very often; it's boring...It's a dilemma, sometimes..."

"So Alla, you have become bored with being right all the time? How do you know if you are right, your intuition? I learn more from seeing where I went wrong. I treat people who are often wrong and because of their defenses, they don't see it until they meet me...Of course, at first they think that I am the one who is wrong."

"My intuition is better than yours."

"Intuition is self-serving. I respect and defer to reality."

"I don't want to have intellectual duels with you, my sweetness."

"Alla, you have other ways of perceiving."

"You can't imagine how different my Angel."

There is a point when one decides to fall in love despite everything. It is like the first time you are on the diving board and you decide to jump. You just have to trust that it will be worth it. I pushed aside that Alla saw sweetness and intimacy in terms of sex. I pushed aside her need to be right and her grandiosity.

Every morning I ran downstairs to my computer to get my e-mails from Alla. What you don't see are the seductive photos and poems. I became addicted to them. Her letters were long, passionate and fascinating. Now they were coming two or three letters a day, four to eight pages long. They were a hypnotic seduction to make her the focus of my life.

My responses sometimes seemed like trance-like compliances. I dialogued with Alla by using another color. Alla often responded with yet another color. Our e-mails were often in black, red, and blue. Alla's words were often in various sizes and in bold to convey her emotions and intensity. Alla had the habit of not ending a sentence. She usually jumped from thought to thought. Alla often used ellipsis...as if there were more thoughts unspoken...

Often I worked late into the night on my paper. Alla was waking up in Saint Petersburg and would greet me on instant messenger. With the emails, instant messenger and our increasing phone calls, Alla dominated my time and my being.

I confronted Alla about our differences. Remember them; they will appear again. Alla could not say that she was sweet, but rather indicated that she was primitive in intimacy. She tried to seduce me away from my wish for a sweet mate, in exchange for a sexually exciting mate.

I was not happy about her conviction that she was always right and that she relied on her subjective intuition more than weighing the evidence found in reality. I confronted her hoping that she would become more insightful in time. Alla was intellectually sophisticated, but childlike emotionally. I hoped that she could grow to love as an adult. I have seen people grow so many times before, but this time my own heart required it.

Chapter 10

The Addictive Quality of Passion

Passion by its nature is obsessive and addictive. There are several reasons for this. When you feel "chemistry" for someone, there are actual changes in your brain chemistry. You have increased levels of dopamine and norepinephrine and decreased levels of serotonin (Fisher, 2000). This is related to states of euphoria and obsessionalism. This biological state of love addiction may be a product of natural selection in that it increases the likelihood of reproduction.

Added to this biochemical idealization is the psychological idealization of the lover. The lover is an unconscious trigger for the idealized mothering figure from infancy. This first love was a matter of life or death. This primitive idealization from childhood is unconsciously transferred on to the beloved whether the love is earned or not. One is never really addicted to a real person. One is only addicted to the object of the idealization.

There is always some idealization in love. In normal love the idealization has more basis in the qualities of the beloved than in subjective erotic fantasy. The more a person is looking to someone else to fill the empty spaces of one's soul, the more that person will become dependent on an idealized love (Sperling, 1987). A person with a weak sense of self looks for love to provide contentment. The lover is expected to provide the person with happiness and unconditional love. That is a child's notion of love.

Our irrational unconscious can just as quickly create as it can destroy idealized love. When our irrational idealization of our lover is stronger than the actual worthy qualities of the person, or when the immature person's expectations are impossible to meet, the relationship breaks down. That is why infatuations usually do not last.

Oct. 9

"Alla I am so addicted to you."

"Great that you are addicted to me...I am glad! My plan! You will need no other drug...People say I can be like opium...I am a lover like you have never known...I am the perfect tool, but only the very few elected may use it...I can easily hold any desire and control any libido...I hate the primitive perceptions of stupid stallions. I don't like a Marilyn Monroe, by the way... T-o-o-o-o-o-o-o sweet for me...I like an image of Valkyrie maiden more."

(Alla's statement that she preferred the image of a Valkyrie maiden should have been a clear warning to me that aggression may become the greater force in her passion than tenderness. Passion needs some aggression for fuel but also lots of tenderness to keep the chemistry from blowing up the relationship.)

"I've dated a few Valkyrie maidens. They are a lot of fun except when they send you to your death and Valhalla."

"I will bring you to heaven...When it comes to love, I do not want compromises...all or nothing...I have ripened for this opening. What do you wish, Robert?"

"Will you dress like a Valkyre maiden? I don't want a warrior but I love the costume."

"I don't wish to war with you. I was stronger and more wise than my teachers. I can compete with geniuses. I am a star here, but I refuse to kiss the asses of influential people...I've slept with whom I wanted instead of with whom it was necessary...

My royal style is too wild! I can't submit to the fools, no matter how rich or powerful!"

(Was "My royal style" Alla's euphemism for her narcissism?)

"Seems like you had a harsh time in Russia."

"Every time I close the door on reality it comes in through the windows."

"Alla, why close the door?"

"I cannot be humiliated and ask for anything. I have an awful character...My motto—If I can't be a good example, then I'll just have to serve as a horrible warning...I dare myself to do a lot of mad, wild things...Oh, Robert, my sweet friend, can you really love such a Siren?.."

(This was a warning without deep insight or responsibility. I stored this concern as an unconscious anxiety. I did not give it much thought. I did not want it to ruin my passion. I worried if Alla will close the door on reality and in the end serve as a horrible warning.)

"You are warning me that you are a Valkyre and a Siren. Well then I must warn you that I am an idealistic rescuer. What a pair. Romantic love is nature's greatest joy and can be its cruelest joke."

"Robert, it must be for you, because of the women you have chosen in the past. I need in heart and brains of similar scale, Doctor...Look, dear, see who lives behind the successful mask of Alla? When I allow to myself to be natural, I am as thin and gentle as a shakuhachi flute...I am soft and warm like a sea breeze...Who will protect my vulnerable nature? My Swan, there is no quick test for true love...You must listen to your intuition. Do Americans listen to this channel?"

My shoulders began to ache badly enough for me to go for physical therapy at the rehab center next to my office. Gene the physical therapist said, "I see a lot of these knots in the shoulder muscles of the programmers. They have repetitive use injuries. Do you work with computers?"

"No Gene, I work with unconscious repetitions."

I repressed the fact that I was spending hours on the computer communicating with Alla. It wasn't the repetitive action on the keyboard, but the tension along with the action. My muscles were absorbing the conflict of my need to love a Valkyre.

"Hi Art, did you get a chance to look at the emails?"

"Yes. I got vicarious pleasure from them. She is extremely beautiful."

Every Tuesday I met Arthur Katz for lunch at the deli in my office building. We met unless Art was in the jungles in South America leading an orchid tour. Art is one of the best psychoanalysts I know. He knew a lot about psychology, but he was passionate about orchids and chocolate. He also adored his wife and over the decades they have grown to look alike.

"Thanks for agreeing to teach my class while I'm away. You will discuss defense mechanisms? Remember that they are just an undergraduate class, not psychoanalysts."

I said, "I'll go over the differences between suppression, repression and denial and their effect on relationships."

"The chocolate cake looks good."

"I'll explain the three levels."

"They are all chocolate." Art teased.

"The levels of defense...I'll take a bite. The first is suppression, which is the conscious pushing aside conflicts and feelings. Next is repression, which pushes into the unconscious conflicts and feelings. Repression can be lifted with insight and there can be a resolution of conflicts."

"Bob, emphasize that suppression and repression are higher level defenses and important for intimacy. These defenses help a person cool off."

"Right. The most primitive defense is denial of reality, which is associated with the most disturbed people. People who use denial have no awareness or understanding of their problems. Nothing is resolved. They end up blaming others for everything."

"Clear enough, but you will need examples. Are you going to Russia?"

"I don't know Art. I'll give this example. My patient had a fight with his wife. I said to him that he saw his wife's criticism as though it was as dangerous as his mother's criticism.

I interpreted, 'When you were a child, your mother's criticisms did damage to your self-esteem. It was dangerous then. Your wife's criticisms are only annoying, but not dangerous. They only seem dangerous when they trigger repressed memories and emotions about your mother. The more you remember and not repress the past, the less you will transfer the emotions of danger from the past onto your wife.'"

"Good example. The last time I was in Russia was in 1972."

"For you dissertation on USSR Jews?"

"Right. I'm sure it's very different now, but bring soft toilet paper just in case. It was like refined bark. I remember paying for it by the square."

"I'm not sure I'm going yet. If he used denial, he would have concluded that his emotional reaction was caused by his wife and not his own transference. I think it is better if a couple shares the same defensive style. Two people who tend to use denial might have a stable but inflexible relationship. Two people who tend to use repression might have a stable and growing relationship."

"And if they don't have the same defensive style?"

"There is war. If a person who tends to repress tries to confront someone who uses denial, each will drive the other crazy. You can't use insight, reason, or reality against denial. Confrontation only makes things worse."

"You'll need a visa to go to Russia."

"They don't take Master Card?"

"It's special permission from the Russian government to visit."

"Really? I have to get permission to go there and spend money?"

"Bob I read Alla's emails. She is extraordinary."

"Borderline?"

"It's hard to know. It could be cultural. She is very Russian. They are defensive for reasons. It is an alien mentality for Americans who are used to feeling safe. The Mongol-Tatar invasion in the 13th century devastated Russia. They swept across Russia with a sadistic mass genocide. Then Nazis killed over 25 million Russians. Stalin killed over 30 million of his own people. This is a nation of overcompensation and paranoia due to unimaginable trauma."

"Hence the Cold War. Would you go to Russia to meet her?"

"Few men ever get a chance to be with a woman who looks like that and is that accomplished. The men that do are very rich. Does she know how much you make?"

"She dated wealthy men from all over Europe. She seemed confused that she is in love with me. Early on I told her my income."

"Did you specify 'annual'"?

"Yes. She calls me her 'Guru'."

"It's not a western culture. She may want to feel enriched by your wisdom. That might be what she is looking for."

"I am so attracted to her but I'm worried about her personality."

"What do you have to lose by meeting her? She'll show you a great time in Saint Petersburg. Just forget about marriage. Have fun. But I can't see her leaving all her fame to come to live in Allentown. How is it that I am just beginning to eat and you are done already?"

"It is my perpetual enthusiasm."

Chapter 11

Repeating Love Dramas

I opened my waiting room door and to my horror I saw Karen and another patient both waiting for the same session to start. This couldn't end well. I excused myself and went to check my schedule book and notes. As an analytically trained psychologist, I do my own scheduling and I alone handle the fees. It keeps the relationship more private, but more importantly, it allows me to interpret patients' unconscious communications about relationships.

Patients can express unconscious conflicts with me through issues related to payment, lateness and attendance. Karen was often late and each time with another rationalization. Her lateness as with most psychological symptoms is a compromise between the different sides of a conflict. She wanted to come for therapy and she didn't. So she came late, or found rationalizations for canceling sessions. Unlike some patients, Karen paid on time. Some patients resent having to pay for something that they were deprived of in childhood, i.e. good parenting. They might unconsciously express their anger at their parents by not paying me.

Karen was here at the right time, but a day ahead of her session. I called her into my office.

"Dr. Gordon, you told me that tomorrow you would be away and you scheduled me for today. Did you forget?"

I said, "That is next week."

"You told me wrong then. I'll come tomorrow. But I'm really pissed!"

The next day, Karen came late and started the session with a long silence.

"What does the silence mean?" I questioned.

"There is nothing in my head today."

"Maybe because of yesterday." I clarified.

"Don't start with me. You'll blame me for your mistake, so what's the point?"

I confronted her aggression. "Do you think anything constructive can come from punishing me with your silence?"

"You are a man, so you think you are right."

"That's an interesting theory. How do you know if a theory is correct?" I questioned.

"I trust my feelings."

"I don't. My feelings are evidence to be weighed along with other evidence. I do reality checks. I make notes. I have you scheduled as usual for this time in my book. I have you next week for Monday because of a conference." I clarified.

"So what? You told me wrong."

"I can do that. I have to be very careful, because I often deal with people's confusion. This happens a lot in my practice. Some people get so angry they use it as an excuse to leave therapy. So that is…"

Karen said, "I don't blame them. This is my last session."

"My patients unconsciously recreate their pattern of conflicts with me, so I have to be very careful, so I take notes. I have a note from your last session that I told you about having to reschedule. You said that you should skip that week because of a hair coloring appointment scheduled in Philadelphia. I made note of it since I felt that it indicated a wish to avoid a session. You got angry at that interpretation. Karen do you remember any of that?"

Karen was silent. She remembered. She was furious that I took away her justification for distrusting me. Admitting that she was wrong was humiliating for Karen. Frantically her anger found another vehicle. It was like her car broke down and with little loyalty, she abandoned it by the road for the next vehicle that came along. Karen's victim status was too much a part of her identity. She went from being the victim of my error (and when that didn't work), to feeling as a victim because I pointed out her error.

Karen said, "Everything is my fault. You only make me feel worse."

I interpreted her conflict; "You must really feel in a bind. You don't trust me but you feel you need my help."

"Sure. Sure. I have better things to talk about than your problems. Will you let me get back to talking about John? I still think about him. Fuck it! It was the first time I was really in love. I met him while I was first seeing you. He joined the staff and he wanted to date me. I told him that I don't date doctors. I was more likely to want to fuck the janitor. I thought I should date him because it would be good for me to date a nice guy who was a doctor. He's from a blue collar Catholic family. At least he wasn't a Jewish doctor. I actually fell in love with him. I was shocked when he asked me to marry him. Then just before the wedding, he got cold feet. I'm glad I found out then what a jerk he really was."

People construct naïve psychological theories about relationships so they don't have to look too deeply at their own problems (Harvey, 1989). Karen thought that if Jewish men would be like her father then the solution was to purposely date non-Jewish men.

"What happened?" I asked.

"He got pissed when the Rabbi talked to me about maybe marrying us."

"Uh, Huh." (In other words, "Go on. You obviously don't want to tell me too much.")

"It fell through."

Karen used the passive voice, "It fell through". She was defensively avoiding naming an actor who was responsible for the action. When patients use the passive voice, they are often not taking responsibility for their actions. I questioned Karen to see if she provoked the situation.

"Did you tell John that you were discussing the marriage ceremony with a Rabbi?"

"What are you crazy? I had to first see if the Rabbi would do it."

"Did John feel betrayed?"

"He said that he might have agreed to it, but the point was that he thought I was deceptive. That was bullshit. He was looking for an excuse to back out."

I ventured an interpretation of her defense. "Do you think you might have provoked the break up because you unconsciously fear marriage?"

"Could be...because of my father, I keep picking the wrong men."

The steel door to her unconscious started to creak open. I further interpreted her unconscious pattern.

"You mean because your father was untrustworthy, you need to repeat the drama and pick untrustworthy men?"

"Sure. Sure. "

Karen admitted that she could unconsciously repeat dramas. That was my invitation to go deeper. I wanted Karen to see that the problem was not that all men are jerks, but rather she might be causing the conflicts.

"There are three ways that people can unconsciously repeat dramas. One is by picking someone who fits the drama."

"I know. I do that."

"But also you can distort the person so that it seems like someone from your unconscious drama."

Karen nodded.

"Finally, you can provoke the person so that he acts according to your unconscious drama."

Karen was quiet for some time. Then she surprised me.

"Do you think I provoked John by not first asking him about a Rabbi doing the ceremony?"

"It's possible."

"Shit! Maybe I fucked it up."

Karen's capacity for self-reflection just took a leap. She was getting it.

Chapter 12

The Self-Revealing Stage

The Self-Revealing stage of intimacy is created when the couple shares deeper feelings, conflicts and fears. The relationship will deepen if the sharing is handled with mutual empathy.

Oct. 10

"Robert, you said to me that you feared that I would be too wild to settle down...What you will do if I shall give you reactions of a child, I just wonder?"

(Again, Alla warned me of her childlike reactions. I did not understand what this meant. I later found out that Alla uses this euphemism to describe her deep emotional regressions, her depressions, her fears, and her rages. She rightfully worried how I would react to them, since I made it clear that I wanted an emotionally mature partner. I suspected that such reactions had destroyed her past relationships. Perhaps she hoped that a middle-aged psychologist would be an unconditionally loving and tolerant parent/lover.)

"Honey, we all regress at times. We have all our ages in us."

"I have no age...I was born an old woman and I will die as a baby. My dear, I understand your fears...It's a normal reaction. If you ask about my nobleness — I am noble...But if you want to receive insurance of my eternal fidelity...hhhmmmm...I will tell a lie, if I will say, that I know about my future in 10 years. I do not want to speak a lie. It all depends on Love...Tomorrow can be anything...Only love defines duration of the relations for me.

I think, my Angel, you do not want to live with a woman who will regret you. You should not feel the pity for you from any woman...For this period of time, I can promise you nothing. It does not mean that I am unreliable. It means that I do not want to be your disappointment. I want that you are happy...This is my main desire. I don't want to tell you a picturesque, cheerful lie. I prefer the iron truth."

(This was Alla's rationalization for her fear of commitment. Alla feared marriage because of something in her past. In addition, people with a weak identity feel a need to constantly define it and defend it. They fear a loss of identity in intimacy. They go from one idealized intimacy to another. They find reasons to avoid a lasting realistic intimacy in order to protect the self from imagined loss. They move between demandingness and dependency on one hand, and defensiveness and distance on the other. It is a constant balance between the fear of losing the object of dependency and the fear of being hurt or swallowed up by the love object.)

"Alla, I wasn't looking for guarantees, but whether there is the potential for a healthy marriage."

"By the way, tell me one thing, my Guru...can't you or don't you want to have children any more in your life, am I right?"

(Alla could not promise commitment, but she was asking about the possibility of our having a child. This was an expression of her conflict between her fear of intimacy and her wish for a narcissistic union with a part of herself.)

"Right, I had a vasectomy ten years ago. Please we need to know each other more."

"OK then...I will tell you this...I feed my parents. I have three jobs now. Sometimes I sleep only 4-5 hours per day. I try to be best at everything. I am a superstar here. My parents are retired professors. Their pensions are just $50 per month! I earn money of eight men, and more. I must be successful...But are other long stories...Do you really want to hear it and again change all the stereotypes in your head about me?"

"Yes."

"OK..OK...I read a lot about you on your web site and you

have shared with me. You may not understand coming from a stable base. I will answer...Russia...I adore this crazy country. But, in Russia many people do not have a normal life. Here survival is a huge struggle. But it is a very, very pessimistic conversation. I do not think that you'll understand me...You are American. Sometimes it seems my heart will become torn and broken forever when I see this poverty...this poor, weak, ill, abandoned Russian people, which have lost hope forever. I have done everything that I can here. I am still very much in the beginnings of my career. Now, I have the best job in city. A few years ago, I lived in luxury with my ex-boyfriend, we traveled a lot...but now I'm on my own again."

"Alla, why must you work so hard now that you are so successful? Is there a point of 'enough'?"

"I suppose, you don't understand—what am I talking about...OK.OK.OK...I feel, you need more information. My Dad's parents were very rich, but I have not received the inheritance. Sorry, I am not a rich bride for you. Unfortunately, my dear I have received only the royal manners, bearing and expectations that is now part of my individuality. Although, I have not received the inheritance, I have received freedom, inner pride, self-respect, intelligence, good sense of humor, insatiable curiosity, solar energy in my heart and a passion for life.

I was first raised in riches. I could allow myself in childhood to choose between the best of caviars, between expensive toys. I saw my grandmother with diamonds and emeralds. My grandfather collected antiques to fill his big house with many paintings on the walls of our aristocratic ancestors. My grandfather used to bathe me in the large pool in their large, beautiful garden near the house, where grows jasmine, roses and strawberries. Oh...A fairy tale life! It was paradise for me. A very sweet childhood...But my father began to drink alcohol a lot. He was very handsome, romantic and very sensitive.

Unfortunately, he was not a strong person. He died from cancer in my arms 10 years ago. I live now with my not native Dad, because my mum remarried when I was six years old. My mum took me from their rich house without money and support. We long lived in poverty and nobody helped us."

"Alla, it's hard to go from wealth to poverty. But the family problems must have been awful for you."

"I did survive. I was the best student. I was always the best in my class. I won all the awards. And my rich relatives, who illegally have stolen my inheritance, envied us. Because I have made my own money and fame without their help, I was a huge bone in their throat. I became stronger and more wise than all of them. I became a symbol of success for young people in this new Russia. Success is the best revenge!"

"It's the best way I think."

"I tried to survive in this severe country without welfare or help from anyone, with only my pleasant face and my diplomas. I have not become haughty, ceremonious, biting, heartless, or spoiled. I hate these qualities! My heart has endurance, chastity and love. When my girlfriends changed men in their beds, as gloves, I studied the world cultures and religions. When, they told me about their unsuccessful marriages, I was studying Latin, English and Hebrew. I studied art, music, literature, and philosophy. Now they are tired and disappointed. I am quite the reverse. I have freshness of perception, knowledge and energy."

"I understand better why you want to leave. You need a nurturing place not simply success."

"Maybe, you are right, I need to work in New York City or London. I don't know. I prefer calmness and isolation in a cozy place, as your house for example. I must admit I love the pictures of your home. You live in a very beautiful place on the mountain...But I cannot just sit at home 24 hours per day...You know my mad nature. I am a big paradox, my Angel. Shit! I want rest and madness...I want different things at the same time... Doctor! My lovely Dr. Gordon...I need some good medicine for my ego! Who can love me, I just wonder? How many men sang songs of love to me? But none could understand me...Will you? Fate determines who comes into our lives. The heart determines who stays."

Alla generally avoided looking into the past. Surprisingly she told me about her childhood. Her alcoholic father was her wounded knight. It was emotionally easier for her to think about the loss of money than the loss of her father. Her need to be rich, besides the obvious, was also a need to restore the life of her seemingly fairy-tale childhood. Alla repressed the emotions about her relationship with her father, the loss of her father and her parents' conflicts. Alla thought that when she found her rich, unconditionally loving knight, the fairy tale would continue. When Alla said, "How many men sang songs of love to me? But none could understand me...Will you?" she was revealing that she is hard to understand because of her irrationality not because of lofty complexity.

Oct. 12

"Alla I feel so much closer to you after you told me about your traumas. Thank you dear."

"My lovely Dr. Gordon, I've never met a person without traumas.

I think people have much more than me. But I think, it all depends on the desire of the person to be healthy and then it is possible to kill any inner monsters and fears. I always had such strength."

"That is what I have been looking for."

"But I am extremely emotional. Sometimes, I am like an explosive. I can be unbalanced, excited and imperious. I have a high level of excitability. I can be fire, melancholy, sadness, even panic, self-grandeur or ideal love. I can be a burglar of human souls."

(Alla needed to be provocative. When I backed off of the relationship, she came on strong. When I spoke of marriage, she backed off and she said that she could not talk about the future. Then she would ask about having a child with me. When she told me how mature she was and saw that it pleased me, she would then tell me how crazy she was. Alla was unconsciously regulating the distance between us. Regardless of a conscious wish for intimacy, the unconscious maintains a range of closeness that was set in early childhood.)

"I have a mask of the strong, presumptuous winner. You will see in Saint Petersburg. I can be the Snow Princess. I am a good actress. I do not allow anyone to go to inside my essence... Maybe, I must to learn to trust people more...It is impossible to open the confidential codes of my heart. I was like impostor all my life since there was no support...I had nothing behind of my back to protect me."

"Your parents are loving."

"Very. But I lost a big part of my native Dad's love, a big part, Robert. Maybe, therefore, now intuitively I try to find the husband—father. What do you think, my doctor? I have my own diagnosis. I know all my problems already."

"Pretty good analysis."

"My daddy began to drink alcohol after my birth. I think mum had an opportunity to leave him immediately after my birth...But she loved him. And she tried to rescue the marriage for 6 years.

She has boundless patience and boundless love.

But she wanted to save me from his illness.

She divorced him when I was 6 years old. My mum married again when I was 9.

The second marriage is to a man who I faithfully love. I live with this pair now. My Dad No. 2 loves me like crazy. We always had a magic relationship. I am happy that this man has appeared in my life. This man is filled with calmness, kindness, nobleness and honesty. By the way, Dad No. 2 is more senior than my mum by 15 years."

"I am glad you have this example of a long and loving marriage. It will help."

"They love each other dearly. Have no fear. I am not crazy. My so-called madness is only good hot fuel for my creativity. Nothing more."

(As with most people, she can describe her emotional symptoms, but without insight into how they affect her relationships. She had no idea that she was describing a serious personality disturbance. She saw it as just "hot fuel" for her creativity. After all, this was her normal. Alla had problems regulating her self worth. Alla needed to extract love from others to feel valuable. She was a burglar of human souls.)

"I guess Alla that a little madness makes love interesting."

"If I can dance the Salsa at top of a volcano and change the color of my hair once a month, it doesn't mean, that I will cut off my ear as Vincent van Gogh. Speaking of cutting...you had a vasectomy 10 years ago? Do you want to force me to not have children at all? Robert, you know already I will have the desire if we marry. I never wanted children before you. What do we do? Our love is madness."

"Do you sense the intensity of our relationship already?"

"YES! Fucking shit! YES! I should forbid you to write and to speak with me, before your charm has destroyed my life. This is my fear: that I begin to allow to myself to love you...I am afraid even tell to you about my feelings for you.

When I hear your voluptuous voice, it makes me drunk... weak-willed...small soft...natural...feel a big compression of my inner secretions and all organs...satanic fire and salutary rest in the same time...Fuck! I need more sanity!

I spend a lot of my inner forces to hold a distance, a cold space between us. Last night, in my dream about you, I was lost inside your arms...O, gosh...When are you coming?"

"Sooner than I thought."

"When, Robert, when, when?"

"I should be traveling to Saint Petersburg at the end of October for about a week. I will need a tour guide and translator. Do you know anyone?"

"Warning! I am the most expensive interpreter in this city. okey-dokey...where do you want to stay?"

"Can you find me a good hotel?"

"The best for you."

"My interpreter and guide must be of pleasant nature."

"That's me the ideal woman...sweetness and charm 100%."

"Must be able to quote Blake."

"Not only...also understanding Japanese poetry, all types of music, lingam Massage, Kama-Sutra and so much more. Come. Come. Come. I can't wait!"

Chapter 13

Personality Disorders and Disturbed Love Relations

I never went to a club like that before...It was love at first sight." William began his story of self-destruction. He was a handsome man in his early 50's, but he looked much younger. He had thinning blond hair, glasses, and sensitive features. He had his own accounting firm, three children and a loving wife. But he had destroyed his life over a perverse obsession. William had been seeing a therapist for about five years during his affair but he was still addicted to the twenty-nine year old lap dancer. His therapy helped him with the cognitive aspects of his anxiety and depression that resulted from his affair, but it could not touch the primitive level of delusional love that he was acting out.

"What kind of relationship was it?" I asked hoping to assess his level of self-reflection.

"First I paid for the lap dances for about two months. Then I wanted to take Tammy to dinner. She said that she was losing money by taking time off from work and I had to pay for the time. She only wanted to go to the most expensive restaurants. I didn't want her to have to dance for a living. So I gave her $2000 dollars a week to live on. I also paid for her cosmetology school and set her up in her own beauty salon. That didn't work. She has no business sense. We never had sex in the five years we were together. She said that she never liked sex. I loved her anyway. Eventually, I went bankrupt and my wife left me when she found out why. When the money dried up Tammy told me that she didn't love me and she found someone else. I became suicidal. I would just stand outside her window. She had me arrested. I can't live without her. I love her. She is really a wonderful woman."

"An adult loving relationship has mutual concern. Did she ever show concern about your spending so much on her?" I asked.

"No. She is a taker. She told me that I had to prove my love for her by tolerating her problems and by spoiling her. That's because she had an abusive father." William still rationalized (made excuses for) her behavior.

I said, "Normally, one would become disappointed and fall out of love with such poor behavior. Instead, you have fallen more in love with her. If I am to help you with this idealization, I must better understand your earliest attachments. Can you tell me about your parents?"

"There is really nothing to tell. I can't see how that matters. I had a loving mother."

"And you are a loving man. But you love the wrong type of woman for a healthy relationship, and you have problems falling out of love when you should. Something is damaged in you concerning attachment and passion."

"My father was abusive to my mother. I slept with her to keep him away from her."

"Until when?"

"I think until I was about 10."

"Perhaps you were her rescuer. " I suggested.

His mother may have used William. Like Tammy, she seduced him without sex. William as a child could have split the image of his mother into a Madonna and a whore. He needed to see his mother as non-sexual to protect himself from his sexual feelings for her that were over stimulated by his mother's seductiveness. He displaced his sexual fantasies of his mother into the "whore" lover, and retained the Madonna image of his mother. I would also need to explore the issue of his castrating father. This would increase his need to be with the wrong kind of woman. By being with a "whore", he could feel superior and not feel castrated. His tolerating not having sex with the lap dancer for five years while he supported her could be explained by his underlying fear of incest and castration. These hypotheses guided me in my formulation of William's erotic obsession.

"William, you seem insightful enough for deep psychotherapy. If you work hard and stick with it, I might be able to help you. The main problem might be that you are not ready to give her up."

"I can't give her up. I really do love her." William said in the desperate tone of an addict. I hoped he would stick with the psychoanalytic therapy that would be needed to help him mature in his capacity for healthy love. I feared that his resistance might be too strong. He was masochistically addicted to the lap dancer. At this point he wanted relief from his suffering and self-destructiveness, but he feared that if he changed, he would have to give up the whole drama and face his internal conflicts.

When we review the five types of love disturbances:
1.   the inability to fall in love,
2.   the inability to remain in love,
3.   the tendency to fall in love with the "wrong" kinds of people,
4.   the inability to fall out of love and
5.   the inability to feel loved,

William was able to fall in love and remain in love. But he suffered from the tendency to fall in love with the "wrong" kinds of people and the inability to fall out of love when he should. And although William would say that he felt loved by Tammy, it was clear that she did not love him. So William had a fear of being loved.

About a hundred years ago, Freud wrote a paper, "A Special Type of Object Made by Men" (Freud, 1910a). It amazes me how brilliant and original Freud was and how little understood he still is. Freud described William's psychopathology as, "this condition could be called that of 'love for a harlot'...the desire they express to 'rescue' the beloved...the libido has dwelt so long in its attachment to the mother...that the maternal characteristics remain stamped on the love-objects chosen later...the idea of 'rescue' actually has a significance and history of its own and is an independent derivative of the mother-complex, or more correctly, of the parental complex...".

William not only suffered from the tendency to fall in love with the "wrong" person, but he also suffered from the inability to fall out of love when it was necessary. Salman Akhtar (1999) felt that normally if love is unrequited or toxic, the love diminishes and there is a grieving process. However, individuals with an immature personality structure and obsessional features do the opposite and intensify their attachment when love isn't reciprocated. They are highly invested in their sadomasochistic fantasies and refuse to accept limits that should have been resolved with the oedipal situation. In other words, children need to learn that they can not possess and control the love object to feel secure and have a sense of worth. They can not "marry" the parent. They must deal with limits and loss and learn from it. That builds ego strength and resiliency. William won the oedipal situation. He won his mother and by doing so lost an opportunity to develop mature love.

William had difficulty feeling passion for his wife who loved him. Yet he had an intense passion for the lap dancer who was parasitic and exploitive. According to Akhtar (1999), people who have problems with being loved have difficulty with renouncing masochism, dealing with "good enough", loss and their own aggression.

William would have to address these issues to be free of his self-destructive "love". But most patients with such love disturbances don't stick with intensive psychotherapy. They often use the therapist as an audience as part of the drama. It is more exciting to live the drama of suffering than to face the reality of one's own limitations and losses.

(William left treatment and came back a year later. Nothing had changed. He still maintained a delusional idealization of Tammy.)

"Dr. Gordon, you gave me a headache last session. It took me days to recover from it."

I interpreted Karen's possible psychosomatic reaction. "You see me as victimizing you. But maybe your headache was due to all the unresolved conflict inside of you. The different sides of you might be quarreling without a good moderator."

"And how do I get a good moderator? You're not doing it."

"As you learn the different sides of you, you will be able to tell the sides that make the most sense from the sides that are self-defeating. You can learn that from sharing the different sides of you with me."

At this point I avoided a deeper interpretation of her transference anger at me. I was tilling the soil for Karen to work through her transferences that helped to destroy her relationships. She was likely to destroy her relationship with me if I moved too quickly. Later on I might ask, "What was your headache saying about your feelings toward me?" The eventual goal was for Karen to have the insight to do a reality check, self-sooth and then act constructively. Now she was using symptoms as an expression of her feelings.

"I can't trust what starts in my own head? Do I have a Borderline Personality Disorder?"

"Why do you ask?"

Karen had many of the traits a Borderline Personality Disorder. She had problems with anger, confused identity and tumultuous relationships that flipped back and forth from idealization to devaluation. I believe that a personality disorder is an inherited temperament that may have been made worse by early trauma. The basic personality is disturbed and this affects a person's capacity for intimacy. Denial is the dominate defensive of someone with a Borderline Personality. Although Karen often used denial, her main defenses were based in repression. Repression is a higher order defense that is favored by those with a Neurotic Personality structure. That is, with enough objective feedback in a safe relationship, Karen could lift the barrier of repression and have insight.

A Neurotic Personality structure is characterized by the predominate use of repression (McWilliams, 1994, 1999). Since neurosis is often due to psychological trauma, it is more easily treated than a personality disorder. But some hard working patients with a personality disorder can make surprising progress in psychoanalytic psychotherapy. It is a long re-raising of a personality. The patient internalizes the therapeutic relationship over time. The therapeutic relationship becomes a part of the patient's self. I can't cure a personality disorder. But sometimes I can help tame it by increasing a person's capacity for self-reflection, self-soothing and affect regulation. Karen might have a mix of Borderline and Neurotic personality structures.

Karen said, "John said that I'm Borderline. But I don't think so."

"It is hard to tell at this point. The important thing is to not be defensive about your problems and to work on them. I think you are beginning to do that."

"I am not defensive. I am very independent. I think that is a problem for men."

"You don't seem very independent from your mother."

Karen laughed, "That's impossible."

"What you call independence sounds more like counter-dependency."

Two year olds and teens are famous for their counter-dependency. They resent their dependency feelings, so they over compensate by rebelling against any influence or responsibilities. Their battle cry is that they are just being independent. Mature people distinguish between a healthy interdependency on reliable people and a pathological dependency that keeps one insecure. Psychotherapy encourages a temporary therapeutic dependency in order to become maturely interdependent and autonomous.

"I don't want to become dependent on you, Dr. Gordon."

I interpreted, "You see dependency as bad, because you

were hurt when you were a dependent child. You didn't get to work through your dependency issues. You are scared of feeling dependent, so you project it on to others and then try to escape from their demands. But how can you stay intimate without allowing yourself to be dependent in a healthy way?"

"What did my MMPI say about it? Why did you keep the results from me?"

"You never asked. Maybe now you feel ready to look deeper. It shows a lot of anxiety and unresolved depression."

"Depression?...I called John. He wouldn't admit that he was wrong."

It was easier for Karen to associate to the loss and sadness over John, than to go into her loss and sadness in her childhood. Ungrieved losses show up later as depression and problems with attachment.

"Did you think you were wrong and you felt remorse?" My interpretation had meaning on two levels: the present and the past.

"Maybe."

"Maybe you might begin to see men without the filter of your father's image."

"My mother feared that my father would kill her."

"What did he try to do?"

"He tried to poison her."

"It is hard for a child to develop a secure personality under such tension."

"She was always on my side. She is a better person for all her suffering. I admire her."

"Do you think that suffering makes a person noble?"

"Definitely. I always had trouble relating to people who had an easy time in life. They are so naïve."

"Maybe you envy that they are just happy."

"Maybe. You feel different from other kids when you were abused."

Now that Karen is talking about the past, I helped her to do some reconstruction work.

I said, "I understand. What do you remember?"

"I remember them shouting and screaming all the time. I used to cover my ears in bed at night. I'd hold my teddy that mom gave me when she had to go to the hospital."

"Why did she go to the hospital?"

"Because of my dad."

Chapter 14

Growing Closer

Oct. 14

"Alla, I don't have many photos of myself to send to you, since I am the one that takes the pictures."

"Why don't you have many photos of yourself, my lovely handsome hero? No doubt, many women lose their brain and heart when they meet you. Robert, I think you look like a sweet, strong, charming, cute, smart, evil creature. Ha! You can collect souls and bodies of women who voluntary sell their souls to you... You are a gentle vulture!"

"You are safe with me sweetheart."

"I do not believe it...Any man, who dares so easily to try to tame me, must be a wolf that has an image of the innocent sheep...When you said to me about your ex-girlfriend Rachel... I felt jealousy. I must admit...I dare to have you as only my gift from God. I dare to be jealous! O-lala!.. I am really sorry, Dr. Gordon. My Modesty is having a nap right now!"

"Luba is a friend that teaches Russian literature at a local University. I asked her to translate some of your poetry. She was impressed with your brilliance."

"My Angel, you have a Luba, Rachel and Natasha. You sound like spoiled old gigolo. You frighten me. I know that Virgo is an emblem of chastity, purity, and devotion. You do not seem like an emblem of chastity."

"It's safe to assume that everyone born in early September has not remained a virgin."

Oct. 18

"Robert, I got your articles on love! URAAA! Thank you very much indeed for sending them. You make me happy with your cute reactions to my requests, Angel...Oh, Robert. Why YOU? I shall try to translate them using my dictionary. Just one thing, your handwriting, these delicate curls of your sensuality; oh, my Swan, it's impossible to read your handwriting without special preparation. I need your help."

"The letter I enclosed to you? I wouldn't be able to read it myself. It is not in English. It's in dyslexia. This weekend I sat down with a pile of your e-mails and photos and reread them and stared at all your pictures."

"I did the same! Oh, Lord. You copy me! I am eating your flesh and I am drinking your sweet juice of love. You are my food for wit and heart. You are my breakfast, lunch and supper. I ask myself how is it possible that I can fall more and more in love with you?"

"I feel the same. It's only the beginning. Wait. It will only get more intense."

"Can I survive it? My first idea in morning and I open my eyes, is about you. My last idea, when I fall asleep, is about you as well...You are my narcotic...I need a big dose of you each day. How much more can it get without my becoming totally lost?"

"I've been trying to write a theoretic article on romantic love. Instead of being inspired, I feel totally distracted from my work."

"I'm not theory. Wait until you have my leg wrapped over you. Take this gift from God...It's yours. It belonged to you for the last 3000 years...You only were not ready to receive it earlier."

"God didn't help me. I had to rely on the computer to find your ad on the Internet."

"Do you know that I prayed to God at night to send me a man that is worthy and fit to be with me?"

"And this is how he punishes you?"

"My dear, the paradise here and now, exists. Even one touch to your palm from me can replace ten wild, sexual adventures"

"I can't wait to hold hands with you."

"I prefer to satisfy the spirit first."

"Fine, I start by fondling your soul."

"Robert, do you want to hear my psychological diagnosis for you, my dear?"

"Dyslexic gigolo?"

"Someday my Angel...you'll stop thinking about your ex-lovers. And you will stop talking about your new love. You'll not share it with former lovers or your friends. You will to hide this and to protect it as your huge secret, because after division of your deep feelings with casual people, this love can lose her true, secret meaning."

"Alla, real love doesn't have to be protected from reality."

"This is very important...I want to smell your heat of desire, knowing that it is only mine. And that I am exclusively for you...I want to think something and have you understand me... Sometimes even finish my sentences for me...I want to know that we think the same on spiritual plane. Do you understand, what I mean...you old gigolo?"

"So now I'm called an 'old gigolo'! We old gigolos have slowed down and now can savor the glances, fragrances, and touches. We give sweet kisses that express the deepest of tenderness. We are sensitive to discovering the secrets to your responses. We take time for your pleasure. Our sexuality is deeper and more multifaceted. We have the wisdom for loving you with body, emotion, and soul."

"Oh, Robert! More! If you know more, than me, please teach me how to really love, my Guru...I want to be the perfect woman, Idol, Coryphaeus for you. I am capable to love endlessly...For the next 3000 years...Is it a sufficient term for you?"

"I'm shooting for another 30 years in good health. Three thousand seems exhausting. Speaking of exhausting, after my flight to Saint Petersburg, I'll take a cab to the hotel. I'll sleep and call you the next morning."

"No way! I shall meet you at the airport. Will you forbid to me to meet you at the airport? As for me, I hate when nobody meets me after my trips. Even if you'll say to me, that you're tired and want to be alone after your long trip...and bla-bla-bla-bla, I know all your subconscious reasons, by the way. I will just meet you and I'll take you to the hotel and I shall leave for home...I wanna ask you a few common questions, 'How was your flight?' or 'Are you hungry, dear?' It's my pleasure to care about you... You will feel my strength and loving calm as it protects you."

"Thank you. What should I pack? Any fashion tips from a pro?"

"I should study your individuality completely at first.

Give me an opportunity to understand—that you want from life. What ambitions should be satisfied? What type of the women you want to tame? Tell to me about your most confidential, most crazy, wild, mad desires. Last advice of your professional stylist, come naked. We shall buy here all new clothes for you."

"Will I look like a Russian gigolo?"

"Ha! Did anyone say you were a little sarcastic?"

"The word 'little' was never used."

"I am sending for you a thousand warm smiles. The autumn and wet foliage in Saint Petersburg waits for your steps...My heart counts each minute. You are mine for eternity."

Oct. 19

"Please my Swan, tell me about your day. What is it like to be a psychologist?"

"I wrestle with demons—demons that live in people's souls. Sometimes the demons act as psychic parasites, so compromising a person's life and happiness, that there is little true-self left of them. Some demons kill hope with depression, some kill relationships with hostility. I can understand why most religions believe in demons and perform exorcism. I tame demons with empathy and insight. It changes both the patient and me."

"I already knew about your work. Please, trust me. I know almost everything about you...Maybe, I was created for the goal to have war with any Evil. Therefore you have chosen me as your assistant...You are just tired having this war in loneliness...My dear, I wrestle with demons as well...I know about exorcisms. And I know the recipes for this purpose...I specially studied it and used for my own body and soul. I have no fear of demons now. I'll tell you about my religious faith and why they fear my fire...Maybe, you'll find your new sweet home close to me."

"Honey, I love your spiritual metaphors."

"My Swan, there are things that are difficult for your western mind."

Chapter 15

Insight

Karen came into the session angry. She was much later than usual. Roy looked up and then went back to his nap behind my chair.

"Are you OK?" I asked.

"Dr. Gordon, you didn't get my message that I would be late?"

"There is nothing on my voice mail."

"You asked me to call if I was going to be late. And I called."

"What did the out-going message say?" I questioned.

From Karen's explanation I could tell that she had left her message on my secretary's voice mail instead of on mine.

As with most rationalizations, her reasoning for doing that only made sense to her.

Karen said, "I am used to working with doctors. I leave messages with their secretaries. What kind of orgasm do you have anyway?"

"You mean organization?"

Her sexual feelings seized on the similarity of the word "organization." Karen's slip of the tongue (or "parapraxis") was an unconscious communication (Freud, 1966; Motley, 1985). It may have been an expression of her Oedipal conflicts transferred on to me. Karen could not finish mastering her sexual feelings and sense of comfort with her father. Now she was unconsciously beginning to work on them with me.

Her lateness could have meant many things. It could have been a compromise between her wish to come and her wish not to come. It could be her need to be in control of the relationship by having control of the time that we met. But by her slip it might have meant that she was trying not to feel close to me. We were working on her fear of depending on me. She might both fear and wish for intimacy with me. Karen was confused by intimacy. She sexualized it. Unconsciously she might sense that the professional relationship and boundary was so secure, that it was safe to begin to repair her developmental arrest. But at the same time she couldn't imagine that the boundary would remain safe. Her lateness may have been an expression of this conflict.

Karen blushed and held her hands over her face and said, "That is such a Freudian slip! Don't you say another word!"

Karen's acknowledgment of this slip was a turning point that would elude just about anyone but a psychoanalyst.

She was getting things on two levels, the concrete overt level and symbolic covert level. She was acknowledging unconscious symbolic motivation. People who are overly concrete in their thinking have trouble with insight, therapy and relationships.

Karen said, "Maybe I left the message on the wrong machine for unconscious reasons. I didn't want to come today."

Karen would rather give me an insight about her resistance, than look at anything sexual. I accepted the compromise and was thrilled by her use of insight.

"Good insight! Why?"

"I don't like feeling dependent on you. I feel like fighting with you." (Foehrenbach, 1994).

"Maybe that's why you fight with your mother so much, to feel distinct."

"She wants me to stop coming here. She doesn't believe in it. Maybe this should be my last session."

Chapter 16

Ready to Leave for Russia

Oct. 21
"Ha Robert, you got the phone bill. So you think now you should marry me so you don't have such a bill? I don't think it is the cheaper solution."

"How can I be without you?"

"What about my harmful habits, mad dances, what about my craziness, my bad whims, my laziness, my love to freedom of movement, my sins, my proud style, my wild rhythm of life, my night fears, my uncertainty, my independence and rebelliousness, my need for a rich existence, love for strange expensive clothes, unsatisfied ambitions, my spontaneous stupid acts, my obstinacy and my habit to hover in the clouds... my habit to make an elephant out of a fly, my need to be first violin, my habit to go against the stream, my habit to live like a rooster in fruit jelly...my habit of hewing down the bough on which I am sitting, and my habit to never tell: 'I promise'?"

"Did you leave anything out? Why do you show me your dark side just when I try to be close?"

"I am not a Miss perfect. Some call me mad...Robert, be vigilant. You can buy a cat instead of a rabbit...My Swan, it is love when you tell someone something bad about yourself and you're scared they won't love you anymore. But then you get surprised because not only do they still love you, they love you even more."

(This was a warning. At some level, Alla knew that she was

difficult. She might have wanted to see if her warning would scare me off. After the initial stage of attraction people begin to show their faults to test if they will still be loved. She perhaps wanted to see if I could love her, faults and all.)

"Robert, I can change my appearance as a chameleon. I can be a child, sex-bomb, ice girl, angel, stuck-up bitch, siren, Cleopatra, or Penelope. I can be paradoxical things."

(Alla boasted that she was a chameleon. This was not due to talent; rather, she had no secure identity—no clear sense of who she was. This is a common stage in adolescence. Since adolescents have a weak identity, they often go to extremes to define themselves through clothing and hairstyle. Alla was very dramatic about her shifting images. She rationalized that she was stylish, because she was part of the fashion and entertainment world. She had no solid self but rather intense, fluctuating personality shifts. One day she was a giving angel and the next day she was an insatiable demon. She carried little memory or history into each ego state.)

"Alla, how do you all get along?"

"If I begin to laugh, the world laughs together with me. If I begin to cry—oh...birds do not sing . It will be nice to shock you...just a little bit . Ha. Only do not cancel your trip to me, please! Do not disappear. You asked me about my crazy style... All my madness is in my love..."

"Honey, could all your madness be in something else? Put it back into the creativity. What do you mean by, 'harmful habits... my sins'? What sins?"

"My Swan, for sincere answers for all your questions I prefer to have warm evening with good red wine and burning candles, face-to-face, soul-to-soul with you. Naked in the bath; I will see a thousand pink petals on the water around me...I will inhale aroma of vanilla...I will be drunk and I will feel taste of your salty milk on my lips.... O Gosh! It's a long conversation...I do not want to discuss it not seeing your eyes."

"Sounds like a good moment for something deep."

"It is possible, that I shall meet you at the airport with

my best girlfriend and her car. By the way, my girlfriend Julia is Jewish. Always I was loved by this nation. Why, I just wonder? Maybe, you will feel Jewish love for her."

"We connect to what feels familiar."

"We can be in masks—Miss Piggy and Miss Froggy. We'll have the bumper stickers for the typical Russian car: 'I couldn't repair the brakes, so I made the horn louder'"

"In that case, if it's not too much trouble we can get a cab to my hotel. I can shower, change and we can go to dinner if it's not too late."

"I told you. I'll take care of you. You will feel my care close to you all the time...Do not deprive me to have bliss to help you, to buy gifts for your friends; to force you to laugh all the time, to make you happy is my favorite act...It's my opium...How do you drive me so crazy Robert? I was inaccessible. I was whimsical... I said 'No!' to many men...I have avoided marriage for all my life...Why YOU?"

"Why you? I usually do not go 5000 miles for a date. New Jersey used to be too far."

"How do you do that? You are a pro...I forgot that you are a pro! Oh, my Lord. I relaxed with you! I shared many personal feelings and desires with you. Now, I know—it is dangerous. Especially with such a gentle pirate, as Dr. Gordon! Maybe, because subconsciously I am ready to be the most beautiful bride on the planet."

"Not so unconsciously. What are your traditions?"

"We go to a special building and sign papers and get drunk. Only recently weddings are becoming western and religious. So where is my magnificent, stylish, white dress and ring with a diamond? I would want to know about the American traditions."

"Weddings here are mainly religious, since it is believed that God arranges marriages in heaven, but the man still pays for them. Did you see the film 'Father of the Bride?'"

"Yes! I love this movie. Can you imagine us as a couple?"

"Our cupids are Nietzsche and Freud."

"Not bad. If this love doesn't kill me, it will make me unconscious!...My brain...my brain does not give me satisfaction. I suppose, my savannah's baked grasses would prefer a good breeze, Robert!"

"Because this relationship is impossible—it makes it so romantic."

"I must admit, I try don't allow to myself to love you like crazy and I repeat this phrase a few times per day. I try to freeze my heart and to block my brain, Dr. Gordon. Though, if tell the truth, for me it is very natural to adore you, my Angel. I try vainly to not think of my desires to you, Dr. Gigolo."

"If nothing else happens, I am so grateful for having known you."

"How are you such charming person? Tell me your secret, please...How did you so easily tame this wild woman? I should have the weapon resist to your boundless charm. Help me! When I hear your laughter, your velvety voice I have only one desire—to force the world to disappear."

"I'd like to take credit for earning your passion, but this is one of those times when irrationality is working in my favor."

Alla was in conflict over her wish to marry me and her fear of marriage. For Alla, marriage represented on a conscious level a rescue and on an unconscious level a danger. Alla's fear of marriage and the denial of her fear was a dangerous combination. How would she resolve her fears? Could she?

Oct. 26
"Alla, I see witches coming down my driveway."
"Are your old girlfriends coming to cook...you?'

"'Stay illusion! Speak to me...you spirits that walk in death'."

"Hamlet! What's up Robert?"

"Excuse me please. They are at the door."

"Who? Are you drunk?...You don't drink...Robert????"

"You don't have Halloween in Russia do you?"

"Ha! No need for it. We steal everyday without the masks... I want to inform you about my preparations for your arrival. I have cancelled all my lectures and trips. I only have one TV show to record...You will be there for this...You have my invitation for dinner with my parents. We'll choose any evening for this supper with tasty Russian food and candles...if you do not object. I have the best tickets for the Opera Carmen...I am a friend with the director. I will give you the best tour of my city. The city was built in devotion to beauty, the dream of Trezzini... I will show you palaces and the Hermitage's paintings. I will tell you their stories...These are the playgrounds of my childhood. We will go to the shops and cafes of Nevsky Prospekt, and show you my work at the Parisian Café. I will give you the helm of the Aurora, my Odysseus...I have a few others crazy ideas for you...I will tell you when you come."

"I wonder what your parents will think."

"They will be charming. Do not worry. I am waiting for you. I pray for you. Perhaps deepest love comes into one's life by walking gently up to you like an old friend through quiet ways—perhaps love unfolds naturally at the start of a beautiful friendship. What do you think, my Alter Ego?"

Oct. 28

"Alla, your Dad and I spoke. I liked his voice. He sounds kind."

"My Dad is very kind. Much more, than me, by the way. I think with age brings wisdom and kindness for smart people."

"I am so sorry if I woke him. Tell him that I apologize."

"No need for apology, my dear. Don't worry, please. You woke nobody.

Nobody at home can sleep before I come back home. It is a tradition. They so badly do love me, that Mum and Dad cannot fall asleep without my presence at home."

"We will have fun together. We'll go slowly. I will shake your hand at the airport and say, 'Hello, I'm Robert. Are you my lovely tour guide?'"

"And I will smile and say: 'Yes, Dr. Gordon, I am Alla your tour guide. Be so kind, follow me, please.'"

"What do you think the odds are that we might not have chemistry for one another?"

"At most one thousandth of a percent. I will be waiting for you. I have been waiting for a very long time. I pray for your safe trip, my love."

"I am leaving now. I will see you soon. I love you."

I was both nervous and euphorically delusional as I drove to JFK airport. For the first time, I saw military personnel guarding the airport. Trauma brings defense for both people and nations.

I felt like I was about to go on a very long first date to a distant and different land. I had traveled extensively but I had never been to Russia. It was strange that I was traveling to a land of former enemies. I grew up with the fears of the Cold War. In the beginning of the 20th century, my ancestors fled Russia due to the state-sanctioned pogroms against Jews and anti-Jewish laws of the Tsar. They sacrificed a great deal to escape persecution and come to America.

I brought along many of Alla's e-mails and photos to enjoy

during the long flight. In addition to Alla's charms, all this effort to meet her created an even more powerful force to love her. I was sure that I would love her when we would meet. However, would she love me? When I was a boy, there was that long walk across the room to ask a girl to dance. The walk back after she said "No thank you," was even longer. I hoped that the flight back would not seem even longer. What will she really be like?

Chapter 17

First Meeting

Oct. 30
I walked from the plane in Saint Petersburg. I could see the crowd inside the terminal peering out. I looked at the faces. I saw Alla. The doors opened.

Glamorous in her red leather coat and long colorful scarf, Alla stood out in the crowd. At first, she looked anxious and then she broke into a smile as our eyes met. She looked even prettier in person.

"Hello. I'm Dr. Gordon. I hope you are Alla, my guide."

Alla shook my hand and with a charming grin said, "Yes, Dr. Gordon, I will take care of you during your trip to our fair city. How was your flight? Are you hungry? Please let me lead you to your luggage."

During the cab ride to the hotel, we easily joked and flirted. She was all that I had hoped for. I wanted her to be in love with me.

Alla came up with me to my hotel room and waited while I showered and changed. As we began to leave for dinner, I helped her with her coat. I brushed her silky black hair away from her eyes and kissed her. It was the first magical kiss at the start of a romance that is like no other kiss. It was a kiss to melt boundaries. It was a kiss never to be forgotten. It was a prelude to our physical passion. It was a kiss that said that we are to be lovers.

We went to her favorite restaurant, the Parisian café. Its theme was fashion. Fashion photos that Alla had taken were on the walls, as well as a large photo of Alla. She introduced me to some colleagues who were at the bar, who worked on TV with her. Then we went to her favorite table.

After enough of charming talk, I leaned closer to her and touched my nose to hers and softly said, "Hey."

Alla stared into my eyes. Tears ran down her face. For a while, Alla said nothing. I felt her vulnerability, which made me love her more.

Alla walked with me to my hotel room. The air was crisp, like autumn in New York, but it was nothing like an American city. Saint Petersburg is uniquely beautiful. The city is latticed with canals. It has story book grand palaces and cathedrals. Alla teased me when I would stop and stare at the architecture. "Robert you look like a child in Wonderland."

It was the perfect fairy tale setting for a fairy tale romance. What began as a whim was now a reality. I was in Saint Petersburg with one of the most beautiful women I have ever seen.

People knew Alla and deferred to her. She was the queen of Saint Petersburg. Besides her TV show, Alla had performed on stage as a singer and dancer. She sometimes sang her words and combined her sexy walk with dance steps and twirls. She was very dramatic, but pulled it off with feminine charm and flair.

Alla enjoyed showing me her city. She was a great guide. She had each day planned.

The day after my arrival, Alla arranged for me to have a massage at a spa. A pretty, young woman took me to a private room.

Alla followed us. She sat next to me and whispered in my ear, "Darling, she is too pretty and you are too cute an American man. I am going to sit here and make sure this bitch only gives you a massage. You are mine alone to pleasure. You are all mine, Robert."

We were together constantly for six days. The first few days Alla would pretend to choke me with her hands around my neck and say "Why YOU?" By the third day, "Why YOU?" gave way to another phrase. Alla would give me the longest and sweetest look, and then looking up, say, "Thank you, God."

Alla studied art and was my guide through the State Hermitage Art Museum. Alla said, "Maurice Denis painted these seven panels between 1908 and 1909. They are about the love and marriage of Psyche and Eros. Oh, honey, I adore his Nabis style! Apuleius tells this story in Metamorphoses. It is a story about us, my Swan! Here Eros—the Romans later called him Cupid—sees Psyche and falls in love with her. That angers Venus, his mother. So then Cupid makes love to Psyche secretly in the dark. O-lala! When Psyche lit a lamp to see who he was, he awakens and flees. You see Robert some things like love are better left to mystery."

I said, "Eros could not stay with Psyche because he was too tied to his mother. So he could only play with passion and not commit. Only because of Psyche's courage do they marry. Psyche is the mother of my science. Psychology is a science that looks at passion so it might stay."

"You will transform me my Guru as Psyche did for Eros."

"Have you ever been this comfortable with a man?"

"Never my darling! And never this much in love."

Alla took me to her home. Her parents were visiting friends. Her bedroom was the largest room in the home. Her condominium was the third floor of a stately three-story building in a beautiful section of Saint Petersburg. She must have had a thousand CDs in her room that went from the floor to the high ceiling.

Alla's paintings hung on the walls of her home. In Alla's room, she had an office area with her computer and satellite TV. Her furniture was of Scandinavian design. There were photos of Alla from all over the world everywhere in her home. We laid on her bed as Alla showed me a catalogue of some of her fashion designs.

Alla asked me to pick my favorite bathrobe from about ten pictures. I had a definite favorite.

She smiled, and reached under her bed and pulled out a gift-wrapped box. "Here is a gift for you, Darling, and a lesson about my intuition."

I opened the box and it was the robe that I had selected. I told her that I loved it and then looked under her bed to see if there were about nine others. I saw only a sack.

Alla laughed, "So you didn't believe me! I see it will take time for you to truly appreciate my unique nature."

"What would you have done if I had picked another robe?"

Alla straddled over me and kissed me. "Oh Darling, I'm never wrong. Did you see that sack? I saved it to show you."

She pulled out the sack and opened it. It bulged with hundreds of letters.

"These sacks of letters came all the time from men from all over the world who wanted to marry me. This was the sack that had your letter. I had grown tired of all the mail and began to throw them away. But one night in September after returning from a trip, I reached into the sack and decided to give it one last try. I had a strange intuition about it. Robert, I pulled out your letter. I saw your photo and read your letter. Then I knew. I knew, but I needed you to understand that we were meant to be. I was patient with you. You will soon better understand other ways of reality, perhaps strange for your American mentality. Robert, I know many things. I know that we were lovers in another time and that we have been looking for each other for eons."

I was beginning to wonder if she did have special powers. It felt like I had entered another world, another dimension. I was totally under her spell.

Alla put on a CD and danced around her room. She danced over to me and slid on to me. Her eyes studied my face as a tear fell.

"Robert, I've never let myself feel like this. I love you madly. I want you."

Alla told me that her mom was sick all week, stressed by the possibility that her only child might leave her to go to America. The next day I arrived for dinner with Alla's parents. I knew that I had my work cut out for me. When I met Alla's mother, she was formal. Alla's father was immediately friendly.

Alla's mother, Irina, was a little older than me. She was elegant and beautiful. She had wise and sensitive eyes like Alla. Her stepfather, Vladimir, was in his sixties, with a head of thick white hair and an athletic build. He was distinguished-looking with kind eyes.

Irina prepared an elaborate meal. Dinner was lavish with lots of delicious food, flowers, and candles. I gave Vladimir a watch and Irina a pin. They were surprised and grateful.

Irina announced through an interpreter, Olga, a Jewish language teacher, "Robert, you are our guest. Dinner will be pleasant as long as no one says anything serious."

For a moment I wondered why they used an interpreter and not Alla. Alla was strangely quiet all through the meal. She was deferential to her parents. The vodka flowed. The food was wonderful. There were all kinds of fish, caviar, meat, chicken, typical Russian salads and vegetables and home baked pastries.

Finally, Irina could stand it no more and blurted out: "Why are you divorced?"

"I loved my wife and marriage, but she was not loving. I hoped she would change. On our eleventh anniversary I asked her if she loved me. She told me that she never loved me, but she added, 'Don't take it personally, I can't love anyone'. She has since remained alone without involvements. I had fifty percent custody of my children. This past summer my youngest child left for college. Please ask me anything you wish. I welcome the opportunity for you to know me. I understand your concern. I am sorry I have been the source of such stress for you."

After asking me several more personal questions and seemly satisfied with all my answers, Irina then switched to Alla.

"You know nothing about Alla's bad habits, do you?"

"I am sure her good points outweigh her bad."

"She will leave you within three years. She left three other men she was to marry. She was engaged formally twice, and ran from them. She is terrified of marriage."

"Maybe because she wasn't with the right one."

Irina continued her warnings. "Do you know about her terrible moods?"

"Only from her over use of exclamation points."

I felt that since Irina could not find good fault with me, she was now trying to discourage me by warning me about Alla's faults.

"Irina, if your daughter had such bad habits, you'd be pushing her on me rather than trying to scare me off."

"Robert, all your answers are clever, but time will tell."

Natasha, a charming Russian woman I had dated briefly, had taught me to drink shots of vodka in single gulps. Natasha said, "I will show you how the Russians drink vodka. If you take the "k" out of vodka it becomes "voda" which means water. You drink it in a single gulp like water."

That suited me since I wanted to get it over with. When Vladimir saw me gulp down my vodka, his eyebrows shot up and he laughed. He kept filling my shot glass with more vodka thinking that my "Nyet spaseeba" ("No thank you") was my just being polite.

I'm not used to drinking so it didn't take much to get me drunk. I chatted on about Russian literature and history. They couldn't believe that an American would have good manners and knew so much about Russia. I think they expected a rude cowboy who would put his boots on the table and belch. We were all having a great time getting drunk and telling jokes.

Vladimir was a riot—toasting to break the tension, and doing imitations of Leonid Brezhnev.

Vladimir and I had a competition telling jokes.

"OK did you hear this one?" I said to my hosts. "The teacher asked the class, 'What happened in 1799?'

Uri the Jewish boy said, 'That is the year our beloved poet Pushkin was born.'

The teacher said, 'Great, Uri, and do you know what happened in the year 1812?'

Uri replied, 'Yes that is the year that our beloved poet Pushkin had his Bar Mitzvah.'

They roared with laughter.

I said, "I'm surprised that you know that Jewish boys are Bar Mitzvahed at 13."

Irina said, "We've been to a few Bar Mitzvahs, but I'm surprised that an American knows Pushkin."

Alla, who had been quiet, had left the table and went to her room. She had been strangely silent while her mother warned me of her terrible moods and fear of marriage. I went to her room and found her subdued and drinking her Hennessy.

Tanya, a close friend and family physician, visited to see how Irina was holding up. Tanya had bright red hair and was beautiful. She was a little older than Alla. Tanya spent some time with the parents and then joined us in Alla's room. Tanya shook my hand and spoke to Alla.

Alla then turned to me, "Tanya said, 'Robert is like Julius Caesar, he came, he saw, and he conquered. They think he has very good manners, that he is bright, kind and in love. They like him, but are worried about the situation, not Robert.'"

At the end of the evening Alla's parents shook my hand, and told me that it was a real pleasure meeting me.

Olga whispered in my ear, "Robert, Alla will not find a man like you in Russia. You are a real catch. Don't be deterred by the mother."

I loved her parents. I could see by how they looked at and touched each other that they were still in love. They both adored Alla. Seeing Alla with her wonderful parents gave me the final assurance. Alla came from good people. And Alla it turned out was dramatic but normal.

As Alla walked me back to my hotel—with the moonlight above, vodka in my blood and love in my heart—I looked at her and said, "Will you marry me?"

Alla stopped and grabbed me and said, "You know my answer!"

"Say it. Say the word!"

Alla had tears in her eyes and shouting louder and leaping with each word, "Yes! Yes! Yes!"

Saint Petersburg, Russia became heaven that night.

On my last day in Saint Petersburg, Alla came at 4 a.m. to take me to the airport. In my room before we left, she said, "Wait. Sit next to your luggage and meditate on your trip for a minute or two. It's a Russian tradition."

At the airport, she gave me a gift. "Open this when you are on your way. I will be watching until I can no longer see the plane. I will be watching until I see only my tears as my heart empties. Oh, my Darling, what am I to do without you? I need to be with you always!"

On the plane, I opened the gift. It was a woven heart and a note that read, "Robert, you take my heart with you. Take good care of it. I love you so much. Your Fiancée Alla."

Alla gave me the best six days of my life. I had entered a dimension where all my fantasies came true. I was in a limerence of love. That is Tennov's (1979) term for the euphoric delusional state that I was enjoying.

Chapter 18

The Romantic High

Nov. 5

"Robert are you home and safe?"

"Hey Fiancée I just got home."

"Oh, Robert!!! How I miss you. You can't imagine! Do you know how much I love you? Do you?...I almost didn't sleep all night because I waited for your call. Oh, my Love...Please Robert, next time, after any your trips, promise to call me any time, even in the middle of the night, it doesn't matter for me! I need to hear just one phrase, 'Alla, I am Ok, I am safe and sound'. Ok? I am a typical Jewish Mum. I need to know everything about my native people. Especially about you. Promise me, dear."

"I will. I promise."

"I had such magical, strange, crazy pictures from our previous life I saw in our first evening in the Parisian Café. I must tell you how God has shown me that you are my real half, my soul mate, my 5th Element, my destiny."

"I saw such deep feelings in your eyes. What did you see?"

"Honey, when I first saw you at the airport and told polite bullshit to you, I thought, 'Fuck! I am half-dead! I melt!' I feel the separating of my brain and my body. Oh, my God! Where is my pulse? I could not breathe at all! Then after 10 minutes in airport, I joked and flirted with you, I knew 'you belong to me. Oh, I am your helpless victim and can't breathe. O-lala! What's up?'

Then in your hotel room when you kissed me, I felt, 'you scatter my ashes above ground and sky. I disintegrate. You are a villain! I am completely mad. Oh, spare me Robert, please! I am in love. Where is my pulse?'

Your tenderness made me drunk. My elaborate, extravagant scaffold, melted. I already felt myself like plasticine in your hands, my Roden.

And in the Parisian cafe, after a few hours of your arrival, when you touched your nose to mine and said, 'Hey!'...I began to cry. I saw many images from our previous life together. I was sure. At that moment I said to myself, 'I am yours for eternity!' I Love You Madly!"

Nov. 6
"Thank you, dear for wiring all this money for me, but Robert, I don't understand—what is this?"

"You were exhausted from all your work. I will be sending you that each month until you come here."

"I think, maybe better to refuse to accept this money. Believe me! It is easy because my royal origin is priceless!"

"It's concern for your welfare."

"This Russian designer, who will be rich and famous in America in 5-7 years, will return to you a big profit someday. Thank you, my soul mate."

"You are an attractive investment. I will take pleasure in my deposits."

"I am the perfect vessel for this purpose. It's a big pleasure to feel strong support behind my back. You give me a magic reliance and feeling of stability. I never had stability in my life! I need you. When you asked me, 'What is the most you have earned in a month?' I never thought that you would send me that. To tell the truth I am exhausted."

"Honey how are you feeling?"

"My Angel, I have a huge weakness now. I should have stayed in bed all past week! But it would have destroyed my plans for your funny and great trip to Russia. No way! I could allow to no one, even myself to break my plans. I used all my stock of internal energy."

"You should have told me. I saw that you were tired that's why I said for us to skip the opera."

"I can be an excellent actress. I can deceive all spectators. I cannot be ill tomorrow! Fuck! All the companies will be at the show tomorrow. People already called me and asked to give an interview."

"What's the point of being an actress with me?"

"When you left me, my organism said to me, 'Alla! Fuck you, Lady! I am fatally exhausted!'...All my sunny energy, all my power goes into my love for you! I remind you that I miss you madly!!!

I really don't know how much you love me. Please prove it to me!"

Shelle my office manager worked hard on the fiancée visa. We made it a priority. I worried how Alla, who was queen of Saint Petersburg, would adjust to Allentown, Pennsylvania. Alla's grand, fragile ego was embedded in Russia and her family.

As much as Alla complained about Russia, she was famous and successful there. Alla could live in Europe, but America was too far away from her over-protective family and social recognition. Alla's identity was not secure enough for her to move far from her queendom. I prepared for her life here, but I remained fearful of her ability to make the adjustment.

Chapter 19

Separation Issues

I f you were killed would I be notified?"

"I would think that you would be the first to know." I laughed.

"Your sense of humor has kept you alive." Karen giggled warmly.

A patient with a poor sense of humor will have problems with interpretations, since both humor and interpretation depend on understanding both a manifest and latent meaning in language. The ability to laugh at one's self shows a degree of self-reflection and acceptance of one's imperfections. Karen's question about my being killed was mixture of her fear of losing me and her anger at having feelings of dependency on me. My joke was also an interpretation of her aggression. Karen's joking back was her acknowledgement of her aggression and an appreciation of my being able to understand and contain it.

"Where did you go? Did you fly? I always hated flying. After the attacks in September, I am never getting on a plane. I can't even look at planes without thinking they are going to crash."

My absence provoked Karen's fear. The recent terrorist attacks on September 11th, was traumatic for all of us. But for people like Karen, it reinforced that the world was terrifying and that she was a likely victim. Psychologically vulnerable people have the most trouble getting over trauma.

I went to Israel in 1991 during the Scud missile attacks from Iraq. When I returned to Israel a year later, I interviewed some of the people I had seen during the attacks. I was shocked. They had bad memories, but there were little lasting psychological effects. If the same thing happened in this country, the trauma would be profound and lasting. The Israelis I spoke to were very patriotic and felt that they were all in it together. They had a strong support system. Just after a Scud missile would explode and the sirens sounded the "all clear" signal, the phones rang. People came to each other's aid. The country felt like one family. When people have a good support system, they can better metabolize their traumas. I was uncertain of the nature of Karen's trauma. But it seemed that her support system may have been inadequate to help her metabolize it.

Karen's long-standing phobia of flying was exacerbated because of the recent attacks. A phobia or any psychological symptom is an unconscious way of saying that there is unfinished unconscious business. Karen felt too dependent on her mother. I wondered if her dependency on her was also related to her fear of intimacy with men (Shaver, 1994). I wondered if Karen felt that she was betraying her mother, by loving a man. I wondered if Karen could emotionally separate from her mother. Fear of flying is about separation from the security of earth. Fear of flying is about being trapped and having to be dependent on someone for safety. Flying is about trusting that there is support. Flying can be a trigger for lots of unresolved childhood issues.

I ventured an interpretation. "Maybe your fear of flying is related to your feeling trapped with no support."

"My doctor told me that it was my inner ear."

That went nowhere. Karen's mother was idealized. For now it was best to avoid the topic of her dependency issues with her mother. I went back to her father issues since they were more accessible.

"Didn't you tell me that your father tried to poison your mother? Was he arrested for it?"

"He left town. I didn't like you being away. I wanted to quit therapy to get even. Then I thought 'How stupid is that?' I thought you might be killed."

I wasn't sure if that was her fear or her wish. Karen was

transferring her dependency issues on to me. This would allow her to work it through and hopefully become more independent and maturely interdependent.

"Tell me more about this abandonment fear."

"It's not about you. When I was four my mom had locked herself in her room since she was so scared of father. My mom felt that father was going to kill her because she discovered his secrets. Mother finally found proof of his affairs. Mom had to go to the hospital after that. I remember it like it was yesterday."

"Where were you?"

"I only remember parts of it."

"Do your best."

"Father came home and found me crying and I think covered in vomit. I was lying outside mom's bedroom door. She wouldn't let me in. I remember her screaming inside her room. I was very scared for her. I was screaming 'Mommy are you OK?' I remember her screaming for help as the bad men took her away. I was hysterical. I couldn't save her from the bad men. I remember visiting her in the hospital. My favorite aunt, my father's baby sister, Michelle, took care of me. Mom was on ward six at Allentown hospital. I work there now as a psychiatric nurse. My mom bought me my teddy at the gift shop on my visit. I slept with it for years. Father left the house soon after that. He wanted custody of me. He lived at Trexler Apartments, apartment 108. I went there to visit him. Thank God he didn't get custody of me."

Chapter 20

The Second Explosion

Nov. 7

"Alla, how are you feeling?"

"Hello my Swan. I am feeling not well."

"I sent an email for your parents thanking them for everything and inviting them to email me through you."

"Thank you Robert."

"Alla, you asked me to prove my love to you? Well...I broke my age rule for you. I would have a child with you. With you, I made an exception about religion. You are more important to me than anything in heaven or on earth. I would never ask someone to marry me unless I dated her for at least a few months. With you, it was only a matter of three weeks. I saw how you had three jobs and hardly sleeping. You were worn out. I want to help you out financially even at this point in our relationship, because I care about you. I traveled over 5000 miles to Russia to see you. I reread your e-mails many times, savoring every word and every picture. I think about you constantly. I totally crave you and hunger for you. The words don't even come close to telling you how much. Rest, recover and feel my love, my passion and my concern."

Nov. 8

"Honey, are you feeling better?"

"Robert, I feel awful. I have doubts that you really understand me."

"Why?"

"You can't imagine, my lovely doctor Gordon, how many efforts are required for my trust. It is a long sad history from my childhood. The reason that I do not trust the men in my life it's not your fault. Certainly, it's about the fault of my native father."

"I guessed this."

"I shall tell you a pair of histories from my past. I hope we shall not come back to these histories. My past means nothing for me since you appeared in my life. I simply want to clear the bullshit in your head. OK?"

"OK."

"Today, maybe I will be as an equal guru for you, an equal to your psychological abilities?"

"Go on."

"I had two engagements in my life. You heard from my Mum.

This man left his wife and child immediately after meeting me. I was the reason for his divorce. He loved me like crazy. He was my slave of love. He satisfied all my whims. Each day on my pillow I saw a bouquet of roses. He fed, dressed me, bought an apartment for me and traveled with me. He almost spoiled me with his big money. He didn't want even see his daughter to not disturb me. It seems he forgot about his daughter all for the 4 years with me. Anyway, I had left him after 4 years. I cancelled our wedding. Two rings for this wedding are still in my box in my table."

"Your point is?"

"Please Robert I must first finish what I must tell you. Another history: I have cancelled our wedding after 2 months of joint life with another successful, handsome, smart man. Another engagement ring is also now in my box, in my table..."

Unfortunately, I saw this man's river of tears. I was like a big egoist. I repent."

"These are demonstrations of love? Is that your point?"

"My poor, poor Robert...You said that you are breaking your age rule for me? I am breaking my age rule for you! So, we can cancel that one. It proves nothing. There were many wonderful men, who wanted to have children with me. I never wanted children. But, I want children with you...I broke my rule for you. This item also doesn't prove your love to me as well. We can cancel it...My religion is my soul. My priest has forbidden me to marry you. I avoided to speak of it from the very beginning, from your first letter to me. I gave you time for your understanding. I gave you time even for your silly mistakes my sweet gigolo...

So it proves nothing. So it was only a matter of three weeks before you asked me to marry you? To tell you the truth, my personal record was an offer of marriage in two days. Do you really think that this item proves your love to me?"

"What does?"

"Just for example I saw in my life, how my ex-lover tried to commit suicide, when I said to him, 'I want to leave you.' To keep me and to prove to me his huge love to me he simply cut his veins...In my kitchen I had venous blood everywhere. I called the hospital...The doctors had to rescue him...That is only one from many stories from my past about how people tried to prove to me their love.

You said that it was only a matter of three weeks...Really? My congratulations to you honey...So you traveled 5000 miles to see me? My Swan! I feel high privilege that I have all your attention...But this situation, it's nothing unusual for me. I am really sorry, my lovely doctor, but I got used to men many times making mad acts for me. This doesn't prove your love to me."

"Are you done? Are you trying to give me examples of real demonstrations of love? This is not about love but sickness. It would disturb you if he saw his daughter? Such selfishness! So rejecting one's child or slashing one's veins are the kinds of proof you require? Do you even know the meaning of healthy love? My idea of love is very different from yours. You have a pretty sick idea of love. Bye."

My dream crashed violently. Alla had an infantile sadomasochistic notion of love. I felt beat up and robbed of my beautiful image of her.

Alla said that she didn't trust men because of her father, but she was unable to use her insights. She had a cognitive insight but not an emotional insight. When people talk about an insight and do nothing with it, it is usually because it is only cognitive. Her admission that she did not trust men did not stop her from acting out her distrust.

Alla felt that proof of true love was a pathological dependency and masochism. A true lover would tolerate her narcissistic demands, irrationality and moods, and make no demands of her. My love seemed weak when compared to her past lovers, who were her slaves.

However, her rage reaction was just after she gave me the best six days of my life. I had trouble dealing with the two images of Alla—angel and then devil. I did not want to lose my idealized image of Alla. I wanted to see her behavior as an aberration and not as a sign of enduring psychopathology.

There are inevitable ruptures in all love affairs. They are either resolved in a way that brings lovers closer together, or not resolved and the relationship weakens or ends. I could no longer repress that I had seen a very disturbed side of Alla. I could at this point only hope that insight would change her.

Nov. 9
"Oh Robert, I could not sleep...Sometimes I even regret

my existence on this planet...Sorry I misunderstood you. Now I see it...Robert, I repent."

"What happened?"

"The reasons for my painful, unhealthy hysterics are very simple. I had a fever and my eyes were swollen from tears...I had no appetite...My body was shaken from huge weakness and in the same day, Marina, called me and without any warning, she said to me, 'Alla, I have news for you...To receive a fiancée visa to America is now even more difficult than before. It will be a huge problem for you...Be ready to not see Robert for nine months.'

I felt that a bomb had blown up in my head! The first idea that appeared in my exhausted brain: 'Oh, Lord, I will die...I cannot survive without Robert for nine months. No way! Farewell, people! I am dying right now! You can already buy flowers for my tomb.' I was paralyzed...My pulse had disappeared. I was broken as an old doll without a head...Understand how madly I love you. I felt that I am lost in my love for you. I am totally lost...I was totally fucked up!"

"I agree."

"Yes. Taking into account that you do hate dependent women, I knew that I am already attached, stuck, pasted to you...I felt inner panic! I had two choices.

1. To die soon without you. Or,

2. To push you away...I took the second way...I thought if I am already in a panic after only four days of your absence, how would I survive nine months? I am sorry, my twin!"

"You devalue the person you love so that you might not hurt so much?"

"Robert, I am honest...I just need more time for explanations for you of all my internal problems, my unconscious fears and, and silly motives...I do make mistakes and I seek to correct them."

"I fear that you are not ready for healthy relationship."

"I would want to stand up to such problems in a mature way.

You are right...I could not have good healthy relationships, because I had no mature concept of love! Only NOW do it see it!...Certainly, I could not construct a good family on such an unstable base!"

"Rather than act out your rage when you are afraid, why not share your fears?"

"Your openness is the result of experience in a very different culture! My Modus Vivendi was formed over 30 years and my coat of mail was necessary for me! Please, understand this!...All my life I lived here in poverty and madness...I showed for you only the good side of Russia...My Angel, I got used to being where each wolf tries to survive and kill another wolf...I had to protect my family and me. This habit, just for this period of time, prevents me to be open in the relations with you...In a personal and quiet atmosphere, I can begin complete disarmament...Be my guru for it...OK?...I miss you so..."

Alla got depressed because of our separation and her dependency. She didn't just miss me, but she experienced a deep pathological sense of loss and panic. She was vulnerable to such depressive reactions and rages because she did not have the insight to help her contain and self-sooth her emotions. She used devaluation against me so she might not feel so bad. Alla needed to make others feel bad when she felt bad. This defense, projective identification, is a relationship killer.

All love has some degree of idealization. However, idealization is fragile if based mainly in immaturity. The idealization can quickly switch to devaluation and persecutory hate. An immature personality views an object of dependency based on needs and moods and not on the enduring qualities of the person.

A mature person can love with a healthy ambivalence feeling both love and at times even hate. A person with a healthy ambivalence tolerates the normal fluctuations of mood within the total enduring bond of the relationship. The love and hate are not split into opposing emotions that redefine the significant other. The beloved does not become a devil or angel according to one's internal affect state. A person with a healthy ambivalent love can consistently appreciate the actual qualities and complex nature of the other person regardless of mood. A person with a Borderline Personality structure (immature personality) swings between feeling grandiosity and deflation of the self, and idealization and devaluation of the other. A mature person has both self-love and other-love based on an awareness of both assets and liabilities that are blended together into a cohesive self-concept and concept of the other. Immature people cannot tolerate the ambiguity of emotional grays, but go to black or white perceptions and evaluations. This leads to idealizations and devaluations that swing the intimacy beyond the tolerance of their centrifugal force.

The intensity of an immature person's idealized love can look like the stuff of a great and lasting love. It is not. The intensity of love is not a measure of its maturity. But initially such intensity can be very appealing.

After I confronted Alla, she was able to hold on to me by telling me what I needed to hear. Was it true insight and remorse, or just a temporary accommodation?

Personality traits will eventually win out over good intentions if there is no follow up of self-reflection and hard work.

I hoped that this would not happen again. People do this all the time with disturbed loved ones. They see each sign of mental illness as an unrelated series of unsettling instances never adding it up into a diagnosis. I put aside (suppressed) Alla's disturbed reactions. I went on loving her and hoped for the best. I hoped that my confrontation might have broken through her denial. Yet, I stored this in my memory. In the back of my mind, I was adding up evidence. Things were not quite the same for me after this.

Nov. 10

"Shelle and I have been working hard on the fiancée visa. It should take three months not nine. If it's longer than that, I'll just go visit you again. Don't worry."

"When? Robert, when?...Come! Come! Come!!!!!!!!!!!!!!! Oh, I stopped warring with mum. She has admitted that she loves you."

"Good news. I love them too. Did they get my email?"

"My parents thank you for your warm letter. My mum is going write to you soon."

"How are you feeling?"

"If to tell the truth, today is the first good day after days of frank horror! O-lala. It seems that the last two days, I had my real clinical death. I am not kidding, my dear. I suppose, next time, I need to accept the bounds of a female monastery. I visited this place six days ago. Maybe, I should have stayed there for all that awful period of time. I am sure that during my war with the Demons, I should be hidden from the eyes and ears of the usual people. Did you see what horrible reaction I gave to you?"

"I couldn't help noticing."

"I cannot describe it to you! Oops...Let's stop here...I don't want to frighten you with my spiritual experiences...I think this is like a Chinese alphabet for your American mind."

"I want to know."

"When I am in your arms...I'm thinking of you all the time.

Warm hugs, deep kisses! I LOVE YOU MADLY!!!!!!!"

Alla saw to it that I never received her mother's letter. She didn't want me to know too much at this point. Alla rationalized her deep regressions as a spiritual experience. She did not want to acknowledge her mental problems. Spirituality can give meaning and support to this difficult life. But disturbed people use magical thinking as a defense. Rather than relying on insight and objective problem solving, they believe that external forces cause and can solve their problems.

As far as Alla was concerned, the problems were over. But I had a bad feeling that I was in for great highs and horrible lows. What formula does one use to measure whether a relationship is worth it? Being in love makes one tolerate things that would ordinarily be intolerable. All things, even tolerance, can be overused. I held on to the hope that Alla would change. I thought it was possible, because I see such changes every day in my work. But mainly, I thought it was possible, because of the irrational optimism of love.

Chapter 21

Trauma and Attraction

I must be in love, because I am more fucked up than usual. I harass him on the phone all day. I ache for him. Don't let me ruin this one. Please! Paul is such a good guy. I love him to death."

In the past Karen left therapy when she was in love in a defensive flight to a new idealized object (Pao, 1973). Now rather than fleeing analysis, she understood that she might kill this new love. Karen was now admitting to her problem of sabotaging intimacy. Being in love this time gave Karen an even stronger reason to work deeply.

"Dr. Gordon, I couldn't stop thinking about last session. Those memories were so clear. I remember lying outside mom's door. Dad coming home...The men who took her away in the ambulance...The hospital...The custody fight...Father's apartment...I don't remember much after that."

"Karen, I was wondering how you had such vivid memories of the trauma of your separation from your mother at four and you have no memory of your sexual abuse at six?"

"That's what happens with sex abuse."

"Repression can occur with trauma, but not with specifically sexual trauma. It's strange. Your father abused you at six?"

"I'm sure of it. I was in first grade and I had Mrs. Harris as my teacher. She was my favorite teacher."

"Your dad abused you about two years after your parents separated?"

"I guess so."

"Didn't you say that your mother divorced him because of the abuse?"

"Sure. Sure. So?"

"I just thought that your mother had discovered him abusing you while they were together and left him because of it. It was after they were separated, during a visitation, right?"

"Yes they divorced because he molested me! They separated because he was crazy. Look, help me with Paul. I need this to work out."

"I think there is something to the confusion. We can leave it for now. But I think that issue is relevant to your current love relationships. OK then, tell about your history with boyfriends."

I left the mystery of her abuse for now. Timing is crucial. If I pushed, I could lose her as a patient. It would be an empathic failure on my part. I could not pursue her sex abuse memories based on my need to solve this puzzle. My questions and interpretations had to be based on what was tolerable and constructive for Karen at the time. I went to a safer history. Nevertheless, I wanted her to keep working on discovering who she was by looking into the past.

"Ha! There were too many! In High School I liked the bad boys. I was rebelling. No one Jewish...Any guy my mom would hate, I wanted to fuck. Dumb guys I could control. I liked to be hurt by them. I still fantasize about being slapped and raped. That's how I come. I can't believe that I'm telling you this. I would only date low class guys...until John. I hated him for canceling the wedding. I didn't want to hurt mom."

"Why were you worried about hurting your mother?"

"I didn't say that."

"You said, 'I didn't want to hurt mom.'"

"You heard wrong. I said that I was afraid to be hurt. You are twisting my words around. I hate when you do that!"

I was fuming inside, but would never let Karen know. Rewriting history during an argument is mind-fucking. When my mother would realize that she was on the losing side of an argument, she would go back and rewrite the dialogue. She would claim that she had been arguing my point all along, but I hadn't been listening to her. She would then walk away feeling victorious. It's still a trigger for me. My own analysis helped me identify my issues before they get in the way of treatment. At these times of my "countertransference," it's best to be silent, self-sooth and get back to empathy. I am fortunate that I had my own psychoanalysis so I could work without my personal triggers getting in the way of my objectivity. My countertransference helps me to understand my patients' dynamics, as long as my personal feelings do not interfere with my work (Gordon, 1997).

Karen said, "Can I continue? Paul is a lot like John, but Jewish. He's an Allergist in Philly. I met him on an Internet dating site. He had an ad, 'Nothing to Sneeze At'. We went out three times. It's been great. I didn't want to have sex with him right away. That jinxes it. Oh God. I love him!"

"Perhaps you are beginning to be attracted to men with whom you can remain intimate."

"I was always able to be intimate. I don't get your point."

"I mean a healthy enduring intimacy. You have two types of love objects imprinted into your brain. Your mother was your first love object. Maybe those low functioning guys were based on your image of your dad."

"I had passion for my mom. I used to love sleeping with her. I'd put my fingers in her armpits and smell them. I just remembered that! I would harvest her scent. I'd smell my fingers all day at school when I'd miss her. I actually...at times...wanted to have sex with her. I had dreams about it. God, is that sick?"

"She was your first love (Fenchel, 1998). Usually, you move on to dad, but given the circumstances you stayed fixated on to your mother. Also your mother might have encouraged your attachment verses encouraging your independence. That might also be a factor in you not letting yourself commit to a man," I interpreted.

"I feel like I'm abandoning my mom. I know. I feel guilty.

She gave up her life for me. I had a lesbian relationship in college. That girl was psychotic."

"It might have been a way to still be with your mother during your separation from her."

"My mother is not psychotic."

"How long did you sleep with your mother?"

"I think until I was a teen." Karen said.

"That doesn't help you to separate and have your own identity. Otherwise, you become too dependent on external sources of soothing."

"Like my cigarettes?"

"Yes, and relationships; you expect others to make you feel OK. When they don't, you see it as their failure and you devalue them. You do that with me." I was interpreting Karen's transference to me.

"Sure. Sure. Don't take it personally. Look my mom is not mentally ill. The stress of my father gave her a breakdown. I think I might have given you the wrong impression."

"Maybe you are afraid you gave me the right impression and you now feel guilty about it. If you continue to idealize your mother, your self-esteem will suffer. You will never live up to your idealized image of her and no man could compete with her. Your idealization of her comes at a high cost. Maybe you can learn to love her faults and all."

Also if Karen continues to idealize her mother, men will catch all the anger she unconsciously feels toward her mother. I don't tell patients an interpretation based on my awareness, but only when they are ready. I didn't think Karen was ready to deal with her anger towards her mother.

Karen said, "That reminds me of a dream I had this week. I was passionately kissing my mom. She looked about my age. I was so turned on by it. I used to actually try to passionately kiss my mom as a kid. Then, my mom tries to eat my tongue. I jumped up and woke myself up. I was so upset."

"What do you think the dream means?"

"Well, I was passionate about my mom. She was a beautiful woman. The tongue thing is freaky."

"Your mother is against you coming here?"

"You bet. She thinks you are evil. She hates psychotherapists. She hates Freud. She calls you guys, 'Psycho Rapists'. She is against looking at the past and dwelling. She hates that I talk to you. Hey! She bit off my tongue! I am not allowed to talk about the past!"

"Nice work Karen. I think you now understand the main source of your resistance."

Chapter 22

Tenderness and Passion

Back in 1912, Freud said, "To ensure a fully normal attitude in love, two currents of feeling have to unite...the tender feelings and the sensual feelings...".

One principle aim of psychoanalysis is to bring these two currents in harmony (tenderness and sexuality) so that patients can love better. I often see patients who become infatuated mainly due to sexual attraction. Some patients with personality disorders can feel sexual attraction, but have difficulty in maintaining feelings of tenderness. There are other patients who can feel tenderness, but can feel little sexual gratification. These neurotic patients suffer more with inhibitions and guilt than the patients with personality disorders.

Without tenderness, the primitive aspect of sexuality (referred to as "sensual feelings" by Freud) will consume and destroy the love relationship. Freud felt that only psychoanalysis could help people with love disturbances. Psychoanalysis could get to the deeper levels of personality to integration tenderness and passion.

Robert Sternberg (1986a, 1999) theorized three components of love: intimacy, passion and commitment. Infatuation has only passion. Romantic love has intimacy and passion. Consummate love has all three: intimacy, passion and commitment.

Helen Fisher (2000) reported that humans and other mammals have evolved three primary emotion systems that combine for love. Each system evolved into its own discrete constellation of brain circuits:

1. the sex drive,
2. attraction to a desirable partner,
3. and attachment.

Freud, Sternberg and Fisher come from very different theoretical perspectives, but they agree that the success of love is dependent on all the parts coming together. Generally, these parts do not come together when people have a developmental arrest in their personalities as a result of early trauma and temperamental disturbances.

I was wondering as I was reviewing these theories if Alla could integrate passion, tenderness and commitment.

Nov. 11

"You can't imagine, how difficult it was to find you! Finally, I found you! UURRRRRAAAAAAAAAAAAAAAAAAA! I found peace with you for my restless soul...I feel much peace, since meeting you! Thank you, Robert...Thank you, God!"

"Thank you God for my computer! I have never been so much in love."

"I wake up with your name and fall asleep with your name. I swallow the opium of your opinion."

"Oh now it's the 'opium of your opinion'? I'm restored as the guru once more?"

"Yes!!!! Oh, Robert! I miss you! I want you, my kind natural virgin Angel. You look like a boundless, fathomless, immeasurable, shameless, pitiless, uncontrolled temptation. O-lala...It will be better to not look too long at your smile...I am hungry for your smile! I am hungry for your kisses...Hungry as a wolf!"

"You can't eat your lover and expect him to be there later."

"I told you, you have taken a cat instead of a rabbit. You didn't see anything yet. Remember our last night in your bed? I took you as a gift from God. You can't imagine whom you have chosen for your life a few months ago on the Internet...In your bed, you will hear my velvety serenades, my elusive whispers... You will feel under your skin the indefatigable mad rhythm of my dance, and for these moments all stars will shine...all galaxies will be merged into one above your head."

"Alla, you are the embodiment of all men's fantasies."

"Only yours...I am real and only for your pleasure...I would want to see your endless eruption and your lazy exhaustion after that...You'll be my first and last best lover, my sole lover for eternity...In your bed, I will tempt, tease and play with you... You will be almost dying on your bed sheets...I want to see your desires, your excess, your bliss, your craziness beating inside me when I make love to you...I will grab you...You know.. I can tear you to pieces! But.. I will kill you softly...You are my erotic trophy...You will feel my pulse and my life in your arms...I will know all your crazy desires, like the palm of my hand...You will have your paradise on the earth, all the days and all the nights of your life...You will fall asleep happy and wake up happy...I give to you all a man desires...I LOVE YOU MADLY!!!"

Alla sent more seductive photos of herself. She was good at reminding me of the rewards for tolerating her bad side.

Nov. 16

"My Swan, my room is empty without you. Even taking into account that above my computer, on my wall, our photos hang and so I can see your smile...My wall is covered with photos of you...and pictures of us...that I stare at all day...Help me! It is not enough!

I hope it will be my last holiday of New Year in Saint

Petersburg. I hate the winter here...I always leave Saint Petersburg at the end of December. I have depression in the wintertime...Already now I see wet disgusting snow on my window...My parents would be very happy if we shall be with them this New Year. I am waiting for you. I am always dreaming how you'll drink cognac or tea in my room soon. I would want to see again, how you sleep in my bed...Melting, soulful, heart warming picture...I enjoyed it so much last time...I sat silently as small mouse and almost did not breathe, because I was afraid I would frighten away your fragile dream...It was the moment of such ideal love to you...I felt an unreal warmth and endless love for you. The sky was open and I saw a dispensation...I could hear a behest of God without the intermediaries. Do you promise me to give me this divine pleasure once again?..."

"I will spend this New Year with my lovely fiancée and her parents in Saint Petersburg. Will that brighten your holiday?"

"Robert! You are a wonder! The world does not exist without you...Sun—is only a flat silly useless sphere in the sky without you...Night—is an awful black gloomy hole without you...All the grand volume inside my heart is boundlessly empty without you...

Day—is in absolute silence without you.

Time—is a fathomless, soundless, ice, cheerless, vain, unbearable, helpless and infinite loneliness without you.

Life—is an Eternal stupid search without you.

I wake up for you...

I breathe for you...

My internal beauty and perfect harmony begins slowly, very slowly to die without you...and I feel myself like a broken flower...

You can't imagine, what happens in my heart and in my head.

The words are powerless...They cannot express even a small part that I feel..."

"You are doing a wonderful job with the English language, Honey. The horoscope you sent is pretty accurate, I must say. You said, 'Your conflict with your mum was programmed by stars since your birth. This conflict was inevitable!' Was I born under the sign of a Virgin or a Harpie? Anyway, I would still rather put my faith in the forces of genetics and the environment than optical illusions and mythology."

"There are many realities my love."

"There is only one where you can find intimacy."

"Robert, tell me about your childhood and your history...if you don't mind. For me, it's very, very important to know all about you...I want to be with you for pleasure and for sorrow as well...I would want to know about all your psychological traumas...I need to know all about you..."

"Luckily—there were no great traumas. My parents supplied me with a model of a stable marriage, good values and the capacity for hard work. I was exposed to Freud and Shakespeare at an early age (and to this day their pictures hang on my home office wall...next to several of your pictures). My mother adored me for my first few years of life so my core personality is solid and I have good self-esteem.

However, I do have two main problems in my personality. The first is my strangely wired dyslexic brain. The second is based on years of trying to please my narcissistic mother. Trying to please someone who is intent on unhappiness is an impossible task. But a child doesn't understand this. What starts in the family as an attempt at a solution that fails, becomes a habit and then an unconscious pattern. This unconscious rescue complex at its best adds to my being a psychologist and at its worst gets me into impossible relationships...Now tell me more about your family."

"Thank you for your story. I remember you telling me about your family history when we were together in my room... I have no doubts that we'll always be together...This is not an impossible relationship...It is real...We are soul mates...My intuition told me.. We'll be together for very long time. The next 3000 years, it's a minimum."

"That's quite a commitment Honey."

"My Angel, you can't imagine the level of power of my love for you. Believe me, I bet, now, you have no idea how much I love you...Robert, I am ready to kill any person who would dare hurt you...I am ready to stand close to a precipice and if you say to me, 'Alla, let's jump down with me'. I'll jump down, and I'll not ask even, 'What for?..' I am ready for self-destruction for you...I would do anything you want. I could to fall on my knees and kiss your feet. I DEIFY YOU !!!!!!!!!! I LOVE YOU MADLY!!!!!!!!"

Nov. 18

"Hello, my Swan. Okey-dokey. I will answer with reciprocity."

"Hello, Alla. Does this mean you will share your traumas with me?"

"Yes. When I was about three years old, a virus attacked my eye muscle. One eye was slightly to the side. And when I was six and eight, I had two very unpleasant operations. At first they operated on the left eye, then the other...They have said, that was necessary to cut the other, healthy eye, that they were compelled to operate on both...Sounds like a bullshit, but it was weak and primitive medicine in Russia."

"I remember you telling me about this."

"After two operations in my childhood, my strings...is that the word?"

"Stitches?"

"Yes. The stitches in my eyes began to inflame...But this operation needed to be performed without anesthesia at all... O-lala."

"That's horrible."

"I felt huge pain during all the operation...I saw all surgical tools as they cut my eyes. They deleted old stitches and put in new ones...Poor hospital in abject poverty, it was awful...I told you, in the most awful critical situations, I begin to joke like crazy...Maybe, it's latent hysterics. My surgeons till now recollect my operation many years ago...I felt such pain and so I joked. They roared with so much laughter that they could not work with me at times...I was the queen of laughter."

"It's not funny. What primitive medicine."

"This story should end very cheerful, but after three years my eye had inflammation...Again I had the same operation... Still without anesthesia...Bad luck...The pain is back and I need the operation again. I have not accepted the decision to do it...I still have the bad, old stitches in my eyes...But I do not want an operation for the fifth time...I am tired."

Alla's reciprocal story of trauma was a warning in the form of a metaphor. Language can express both conscious and unconscious messages at the same time. She gave me a story of medical trauma that avoided the issues of her psychological traumas with her father and her problems with her past lovers. Nevertheless, her story revealed that people who were to help her see had hurt her. She trusted and she was let down. She felt worn out and did not want to see any more scalpels (psychological or otherwise).

I showed Alla's email to an eye surgeon friend of mine. He was horrified at her description of her surgeries. He agreed to correct her problems when she came here to live. That was one of many surprises I had in store for Alla.

Nov. 20

"Robert, my Love I think, the first period after I come to the USA, it will be very difficult for me...I am ready to have psychological war with my ego and my habits...Many of my friends, who left to live in USA, already many times told me, 'Alla, be ready for disappointment...You got used to urban life. You lived in Saint Petersburg and crazy Moscow...You really love the noisy life with night cafes, restaurants, bars, and bright show-windows of the huge shops...You were bored in Helsinki... It was a too quiet and boring atmosphere for you...In many small American cities there is no nightlife at all. Be ready...Everyone sits at home and people do not go for walks on the streets. For the first period of time you will think that you are in a deep trap...Be ready...It's real horror for the Russian mentality...Take medicine for depression for the first three months...We promise that you will feel like you are dying slowly.' I guess they want to frighten me...I will try to be more optimistic than my friends! And I will have you on my side."

"Your friends are discouraging for their own reasons. If it were so bad here, why are so many people trying to come to the United States? Also remember that you will not have their financial problems. Besides people get depressed over relationships not the lack of a night life."

"Thank you my Swan. I have no reason to worry about coming to America. I trust you. I adore you and I cannot live without you anyway...I have the main purpose to make you the most happy husband on this planet...For the first period I want not to have to work and be feminine and lazy...Are we rich enough for it?"

"We are rich enough."

"I can't wait to shop in New York, my Swan. I only do not know how much time you can spend with me...Robert, tell me, please, about your usual workday."

"I work long hours. It will be necessary if you wish to be feminine and lazy and shop."

"I see you are really a busy person. Tell me, please, how many hours you can spend with me within one work-week?"

"I work about 10 hours a day, for about five days."

"What will I do? I will die without you."

"Alla, my Russian friends here spoke of the necessity to drive here. I noticed how you always take cabs."

"I can't drive. I finished special lessons for a driver's license. That was eight years ago...I had the examination for this and I received very weak grades. I am an absent-minded and inattentive woman...Maybe, I was afraid to drive on the Saint Petersburg streets...You remember the crazy atmosphere among Russian drivers? Maybe, I need a bicycle for first few months!.. It will be a big scandal in your city...'People, who is that crazy teenager in multicolored clothes on a bicycle? Who? Dr. Gordon's wife? Bullshit! I can't believe it!'"

"I will teach you to drive on the American streets. It is much easier than trying to drive in Russia. Unlike Russians, most Americans actually follow the driving rules and are sober. I made plenty of closet space for you and I gave Shelle, my great office manager, most of my antique furniture. I know you don't like antiques. You can redecorate and make it your home. I have many wonderful surprises in store for you."

"You are wonderful. I adore you. I can't wait! As for me, I'm going to rape you in the airport."

Chapter 23

Pants Frozen in Time

Karen came into the office and looked around. "Where's Roy?"

"He's at the groomers."

"My mother drives me crazy. We got in a big fight. She loves pepperoni pizza with thick crust. I heard her order pizza. When the guy brought a regular pizza, she asked 'where is the pepperoni?' He said, 'You didn't order pepperoni'. My mom shouted, 'I did!' She sounded just like I can get. It's scary to hear myself through her. The guy went back and got one with pepperoni. She said real loud, 'Dumb guy; won't admit he's wrong'. I said, 'Mom you didn't say 'pepperoni''. So then she accused me of siding with him because he's a man. We had a huge fight right in the pizza place. I stormed out. We're not talking."

"I don't remember hearing about such a bad fight before. It must have been very upsetting."

"It is typical. Before that she told me that she now wants me to get her the pants I wanted to get her at Neiman Marcus in Philly. That was two months ago."

"The size eight."

"What a memory you have! The world has to be on hold for her until she decides what she wants. She thinks those pants are just waiting for her. And she constantly confuses when she had thought something with having said it. She can't get it straight if she said it or thought it. It happens all the time. I've been depressed. I'm not sure why."

I interpreted, "When that frustrated anger bounces up against your idealization of your mother, you could get depressed."

This is an interpretation of depression as anger redirected towards the self. Depression can come from the loss of an object of dependency, loss of love or chronic empathic failures. But it also can come from anger turned against the self. When a child feels anger toward a parent, the child may fear the destructiveness of his or her own anger and redirect it towards the self. This both protects the parent and punishes the self (Jacobson, 1971).

"I feel so protective of my mother."

"How did you get burdened with that job?"

"My mom would tell me in bed as we cuddled to never leave her. I feel so responsible for her."

"That's an unfair and irrational burden that hurt your ability to love a man without guilt," I said.

"I guess so. You know I was thinking how much I miss Aunt Michelle, my father's sister. She would baby-sit me. She was so loving. After my father left, my mom told her not to come around. I think I will try to contact her and see what I can find out about my past."

Chapter 24

Explosion Number Three

Dec. 6

"Robert, I got your INS papers."

"I wanted you to see what I sent to the Immigration and Naturalization Service for your fiancée visa."

"I feel like a stupid clown, who could understand and read Fromm's 'Anatomy of Human Destructiveness' in one day as a teenager, but this...I have a lot of questions to you, a lot of stupid questions...I am sorry, my dear...When I started to read your papers, it seems, honey that I have returned thirteen years back, when I began to study Jewish hermeneutics...I just want to say that I am not interested in your past...It is your sacred territory...But I am interested to know about your current situation...I remember, you told me long ago and again in your hotel room how much you made and lots of stuff about it..."

"You are doing a lot of dancing."

"OK.OK...Anyway, the poverty does not frighten me...I believe in love and paradise in a hut...I love you Honey!"

"What's this about poverty?"

"I am confused about how much you really make..."

"I told you from the very beginning what I made. I told you again during my visit. I didn't want you have any misconceptions. I am not an aristocrat and I don't own factories, but there is no need to worry about money. You can ask me anything about my past, my present, or our future."

"Do you understand my sincere motive? I hope so!.. Maybe,

for my goals and crazy dreams, I shall be compelled to work immediately in USA?"

"If you wish, I think it is good to work and have your own money. But why are you acting like I am poor?"

"When you told me your income, it seemed like a lot...But you didn't tell me that a third of that goes to taxes!"

"My life style is upper middle class. I make more than 98% of Americans based on my taxable income from my private practice. Are you surprised that I pay taxes? Americans actually pay taxes, unlike the Russians. But then again our streets do not have giant holes, our bridges are not crumbling and most things work here."

"Robert, please, I need more details. What are your expenses? May I ask? Please don't be angry..."

"It's there in the papers. Why are you worried?"

"I have been drinking all evening. Robert, how can you do it? It is impossible to afford this crazy woman with rich tastes and perhaps soon a child with such funds! How can we do anything that you promised me? You told me such bullshit. You shattered all my iridescent dreams. All my dreams you shattered. How can we travel? How can we return to Russia often? How can we do any of what you promised me? How could you have told me such bullshit? You are not the person I thought you were."

"I was honest with you. Why do you assume I lied? How much have you been drinking? Do you drink when you are upset? I make enough so you do not have to work, if you do not wish it. But that means there are limits to my funds. If I do not make enough money for you, please be honest with me. I would rather our relationship end now, than to fight about money and then divorce. Didn't you just say that you would live in a hut with me?"

"I did not mean to offend you, but how is it possible to live on such funds? Why did you say bullshit to me?"

"I never lied to you. I never misled you."

"Robert, when you told me your income you didn't mention that one third goes to taxes! That's a big difference! It is not enough! You boasted to me. I know it is your way. But now I know that it is not what you promised."

"First, I had to prove my love for you, and it wasn't enough. Now it's not enough money. It's 'never enough' with you. It's not my job to try to satisfy all your needs. They are insatiable. Don't assume that I am untrustworthy. Don't punish me for the sins of your father. Your fear of betrayal and poverty is about your childhood, not me. You go into a rage at the slightest provocation. Your mother said that you have terrible moods. I see them. Your mood swings define me. When you are feeling good, I am deified. When you feel frightened, or depressed, I am demonized.

Can you have a mood disorder? This worries me. I will be very understanding of your problems as long as you have insight and take responsibility for them. Take a hard look at yourself before you go accusing me of being a liar. I am at this point prepared to cancel my trip to Russia. It's up to you."

Dec. 7

"I didn't have trauma in my childhood. You think that I try to punish you for the sins of my father?.. Such a stupid phrase...It was never a conversation about fucking money. I don't care about money. Fucking bullshit!...I did not accuse you of deception. When you spoke of your income it sounded like a lot for me...You think that I can understand all this fucking money-stuff? When I have seen your business papers, I saw that I did not take into account your taxes and expenses...I thought when you told me your income that was how much money we had to spend...I was drunk...But do not suspect me of alcoholism! Do not diagnose me!!!...Save the diagnosing for your fucking patients and for yourself!!! My best friend forgives even my terrible moods. Your remedy may be worse than the disease!!! Thank you for diagnosis of a mood disorder...Another miss!!! How can you get paid for such poor psychology?"

"Fuck You Alla! You have a lot of nerve! How on earth did you think that I would be spending all my income just for you? Are you the only expense that I am allowed? You can be in denial about your problems with distrust and anger all you want. But your denial doesn't work on me. You say that it is not about money, but it is. You said that it had nothing to do with your past, but it does. You said that it is not about distrust, but it is. This is your third explosion in two months. You don't think that something is wrong with you, but there is."

"I am prepared, that you will cancel your trip to Russia and end our relations."

Dec. 9

"Hello, my Swan, I didn't understand how my words disgustingly sounded on the phone. I had no the right to accuse you without proof...It was my fault. I am sorry, Robert...I repent...You know my temper...I am like dynamite sometimes... Only one spark can incinerate everything around like a bomb. I regret my words...But please don't ever say 'Fuck you, Alla' any more please. Honey, never, nobody dared to allow to say such a disgusting phrase to me...Never in my life...I was shocked...This is a deep, awful insult for me...Do you understand what it means for me, honey?"

"I don't need to use those words. I hope that doesn't become the focus."

"Don't do it again? OK? Your anger is awful as well, honey! Thank heaven I love you beyond belief. After all these tests, I must admit, I love you more than ever. Please forgive me, my Love."

"I forgive you."

"You already live inside me...Deep, deep inside me...We only measured the depth of this feeling...We only measured the depth our love, Honey...Nothing more...It's not conversation on money or past or anything...On Friday, I was like bottle-screw... Even if you will see my blind rage...Even if you will feel my crazy resistance...I'll be on your side. I am with you...My heart belongs to you. If you will see that I have unreasonable fears or other problems, you will correct me. I would recommend to do it tête-à-tête, face-to-face and then you can supervise my process and my reactions. Please...softly...softly, my Swan. I would recommend do it naked with sweet kisses; deal?"

"Deal."

"Robert, I know you want to make contacts with psychologists, and perhaps lecture here. I have already taken care of this many weeks ago. I am very proud to have acquaintance with a well respect psychologist whose name is Nadya. I have visited her after your departure from Saint Petersburg and told about our love story (Sternberg, 1999). She saw photos of you. She read your articles. I told her that you can bring the big knowledge to this city. Perhaps you will open a practice with her here. I have prepared this base for you. We have arranged for your grand lecture in Saint Petersburg. You are invited to be the honored guest lecturer on December 26 at the Saint Petersburg Medical University. Already there are over 100 psychologists, psychiatrists, students and professors of medical institute signed to hear you. It will be a new intellectual adventure for you."

"It will be fun. I will lecture on love relations."
"You can use us as an example!"

Alla's fluctuating personality enabled her to move away from this terrible fight faster than it started. She felt that it had no meaning other than it was a misunderstanding. The problem of her distrust, anger, and fears were shifted to my anger as the problem.

Since Alla often used the phrase "Fuck you!" I did not expect her degree of moral outrage. But her grandiosity would not tolerate the same words said to her. I had no idea that those words would become the main issue. The issues of Alla's rage, fears, and distrust were not really resolved, but swept under the romantic rug. However, Alla was able to apologize. Her mother later told me that Alla only just began to apologize since my appearance in her life.

Later, Irina told me that after Alla returned from Finland this past August, she was very depressed about the ending of a relationship there. She saw Nadya for a few sessions. Alla didn't want me to know that she had been in therapy and had been on medication. She gave me the impression that she knew Nadya only as a friend.

Alla just wanted to move on and forget our fight. For her it was only a test of love. She said that it even made her love me more. Our conflicts fit into her unconscious drama. I still loved her, but I didn't love her more. All this drama didn't sit well with me. It was not the same anymore. Since Alla had little insight into her behavior, I feared that the pattern would repeat itself.

Chapter 25

Self-Reflection and Memory

I had a big fight with Paul. He called me 'inconsiderate'!"
Karen's ego was still fragile. She projected a lot of aggression onto his comment, which was probably correct. It was Karen's habit to use something like this as a rationalization to leave a relationship. She needed her intimacies to provide a constant source of affirmation and security. When her object of attachment did not reinforce her image of the lovable perfect child, she crumbled and raged. Karen was dependent on her narcissistic feedings.

"Paul said that on Saturday he felt angry since his friends were waiting over an hour because I was late. We had to find another restaurant since we lost our reservation. I didn't know he was upset until the end of the night. I asked him what was wrong. He told me that I was inconsiderate for being so late and acting so nonchalant about it. I was furious. I thought 'how dare he criticize me?' I was ready to end it. But the next day, I called him. I didn't want to lose him, but I was still angry with him. I didn't think it was such a big deal. When I called him I told him that I forgave him for being so intolerant. Well that made things worse. He dared to say that I was self-centered, inconsiderate and defensive."

"Karen, I know how sensitive you are to criticism, but it's important to learn to take constructive feedback if you wish to have a healthy relationship."

"I told him that he was not my psychologist."

"Being your psychologist hasn't made it any easier for me."

"Don't be smart."

I said, "Couples can share psychological insights without being psychologists. The point is if the feedback is fair and constructive" (Bergmann, 1995).

"I remembered you telling me, 'You fight to feel understood. You don't fight to get someone to see things your way.' I called him back...after I had hung up on him.... I realized I was acting like my mom. My mom does that all the time. She does something so inconsiderate and when you say something about it, she makes your anger the problem. All that talk about my mom helped. I was able to see that I was copying her. I actually said that I was sorry. I used to think that admitting that I was wrong was an utter defeat; that I was worthless if I were wrong. But he was thrilled that I could see my problem and could say that I was sorry. I couldn't do that with John. Now I can do that...So is the couch better?"

Karen was beginning to internalize our relationship into her personality. She remembered interpretations and insights and applied them in a critical situation. She was starting to break old self-defeating dramas (Williams and Schill, 1994). Karen understood that her mother did not want her to go deep into herself. But therapy was helping her to have a better relationship with her boyfriend. Now Karen wanted to go deeper.

Freud as a neurologist initially used a couch for physical examinations. Eventually he discovered that listening to patients' stresses revealed a great deal more about their symptoms than the physical exam. When the patients were reclining they were able to freely think, or associate to connections between their symptoms and the traumatic events or conflicts that caused them. Eventually the analytic couch became associated with classical psychoanalysis. Today many analytically oriented psychotherapists make use of the analytic couch to promote deeper self-reflection (Stern, 1978).

"It used to be used for deep regression, now it's more for focus. Let me demonstrate. Karen how many door knobs do you have in your home?"

Karen moved her eyes from me to somewhere above her head and to the side.

"I don't know. Do I include the outside doors?"

"Doesn't matter. You did it already. Where did you look?"

"Up and to the side."

"You defocused me. Usually you stare at my face in search for non-verbal cues about what I am feeling. But this time my facial expressions were irrelevant and a distraction to the question about the doorknobs. You unconsciously looked away from me to begin to remember and count your doors."

"If I use the couch will I focus more on my memories?"

I said, "Memories and feelings...In counseling, the patient sits up and looks to the therapist for advice to handle a problem. In psychoanalytic therapy the patient looks inward with the guidance of the analyst. Using the couch helps you self-reflect without the defenses and habits of usual conversation. Self-reflection is an important component for personal growth" (Hoglend, 1994).

A national survey of psychologists who themselves went for therapy were asked what they looked for when seeking treatment for their problems. They ranked insight and personal growth higher than symptom reduction. This was regardless of their theoretical orientation. Even cognitive behavior therapists, who do not emphasize insight in their own work, wanted to have insight therapy for themselves (Pope and Tabachnick, 1994).

Karen looked to the couch and said, "When can I start?"

Karen surprised me. When Karen came into treatment she only wanted advice. Now she wanted personal growth. Karen had worked through enough of her resistances to start deeper work. Karen was becoming a patient in psychoanalytic therapy.

"Karen, just lie down and feel free to say anything as long as it has emotion."

"You told me that twice a week therapy is much more than twice as powerful...how about more than that?"

"People have a strong need to vent and tell what happened

to them during the week. They want support and guidance. There is often too little time once a week for deeper exploring into personality. With twice a week there is more time for exploring personality and transferences. A three to four day a week psychoanalysis explores more areas of the unconscious with the goal of a significant maturation in personality."

"Can't you over analyze everything?"

"That's not using constructive self-reflection. That's obsessing and going nowhere. Don't confuse the two."

"How can I tell the difference?"

"Obsessing is circular. It goes nowhere and gives nothing but anxiety. Self-reflection lets you understand yourself so that you can deal with life better."

"OK. Do I just lie down here?"

"Sure, Karen just like it was a couch. Try not to censor your thoughts."

"There is nothing there."

I said, "That means you are trying not to think of anything."

"It needs to be reupholstered and the springs are bad. (Long silence......) I used to have headaches all the time. Now I can't remember the last time I had one. I would hate to think that was because of the therapy."

"Imagine if you had to give someone credit for helping you. Please go on."

"...I remember something to talk about. I had another one of my sick dreams. Just promise not to send me away. OK?"

"Like the bad men who took your mother to the mental hospital?" I interpreted.

"Maybe...they were just doing their job as you are."

"It seems like you are blaming less and are seeing men more objectively."

"Yes. You don't seem as nasty Dr. Gordon...maybe even nice sometimes."

Karen's transference to me was changing. This should generalize to her relationships with men.

"Your view of men might be changing. Tell me about your dream."

"I was kissing a guy in the dream. I think he was Paul. I'm not sure. Then he turns into a spider. She wraps me in her web. I feel trapped and terrified. The spider is going to eat me."

"She wraps you? What's your association to the dream?"

"I said 'She'? I have a spider phobia."

Spider and snake phobias are so common that many psychologists believe that the repulsion to them is a result of evolution that is hard wired into our brain.

But why would many more women than men have spider phobias (Bourdon, 1988)? Some analysts think that because women feel too identified and tied to their mother, they feel trapped in her web if the mother is psychologically parasitic. Research shows that phobias are correlated to neuroticism (that is general insecurities) and rarely from a particular trauma with the phobic trigger (being hurt by a spider for example) (Mulkens, de Jong, and Merckelbach, 1996).

Even if the phobia is tied to a particular event, that event is an emotional last straw and becomes a symbolic focal point. Phobias may be symbolic of an internal conflict that is projected on to a situation or object. Karen also had a phobia about flying. Both the spider phobia and the flying phobia at the very least were an expression of Karen's feelings of vulnerability.

Dreams and phobias are both the result of the same process of the symbolization of unconscious conflicts or traumas. I interpret them all the same, as the language of the unconscious telling me that something is wrong and in need of understanding. Research shows that trauma will affect the content, repetition and intensity of dreams (Esposito, 1999; Hartman, 2003).

"What's the action in the dream?" I asked. It is easier to understand a dream by its verbs than by its nouns. Verbs are hard to disguise.

"First I'm kissing Paul and then the spider tries to eat me. Hey it's like the other dream I told you about my mother eating my tongue."

"It's a repetition of a theme."

"I feel my mom eats me up. Hey, remember you said that I feel guilty being with a man because of my mom. Is that why Paul turns into her?"

"I think so. Maybe you fear that Paul will turn into your mother and eat up your identity. You fear that's what happens when you get close." I interpreted.

"God, you're right. Maybe my fear of being with men is because I'm afraid that I will be leaving her. I can't leave her and I'm afraid to get close to anyone else."

"Karen, fathers help children leave their mother and get ready for the world of others."

"How come I don't dream about my father?"

"I don't know. Karen you said that your father molested you during a visit, after your parents were separated. How did your mother know you were molested?"

"I don't remember...Wait...I think mom was bathing me. My vagina was red. It burned in the water...She called her lawyer. They took me to a therapist. The therapist testified in court that I was molested...My mom said that because the judge was a man, he said that there wasn't enough evidence to put my father in jail...I refused to see my father after that. I never saw him again...Do you have another time after 3? I'm ready for three times a week on the couch. I have to get in shape. I want to marry Paul."

"I think I have another time for you at 3:15 on Fridays."

"That's not good. That's when I go to visit my mom. Do you have another time?"

"Even if I did, there is something of symbolic value here."

"How can another time be symbolic?"

"You can see your mother an hour later. By your dreams and your symptoms it seems that you have sacrificed your relationship with men because of your unhealthy attachment to your mother. I think you need to consider that self-interest is not being selfish. You need to have your own life."

"I thought my problems with men were due to my father."

"That was my initial assumption. But as I listened to you, it seems it might have first started with the kind of attachment you had with your mother. The trauma with your father came on top of a weak foundation."

"I'll take the Friday appointment, but I'll have hell to pay for it."

Chapter 26

The Second Trip To Russia

On December 23, I left for Russia. The icy weather brought on long delays. I was stuck at Moscow's cold dreary local airport for 12 hours waiting for information about my connecting flight to Saint Petersburg. I took out my lap top and I worked on my lecture until my battery gave out. It was the most unlikely place for a break through in my thinking. I finally found a way to bring together an integration of theories of love into one meta-theory. Ayala Malach Pines (1999) called for an integration of evolutionary theory, psychoanalytic theory, social norm theory and social construction theory in her superb review of the factors of why we choose the sort of lovers we do. I found the way to do it while freezing in Moscow.

I noticed a large rugged looking man with light hair about my age reading a novel in English. I walked over to him and asked, "American?"

"No, Australian."

"It's miserable here. I can't get any information about the flight. Do you know anything?" I said.

"They don't know themselves. It's too icy for the planes. Look at the Russians. They brought blankets and food. They are used to delays and no information. Only the foreigners are pacing. Relax. What are you doing in Russia?"

"Visiting my fiancée."

"Me too. I wonder if we used the same Internet service."

We hadn't, but our fiancées lived near one another and we

made a date to all get together in Saint Petersburg. Later I met a Russian boy about my son's age coming back from Germany. He overheard me speaking English and asked if he could practice his English with us.

"Russian women make fine wives, if you get good one." The boy advised.

I laughed, "But you won't really know if she's a good one for some time."

"Can't you use psychology and tell right away?" the boy asked. I often get this after telling people that I am a psychologist.

"Sometimes, all traits come out in time. Some things come out sooner than others. Anxiety is hard to disguise."

"Everyone has anxiety," the Aussie said. "It helps sell beer."

"Anxiety is often a signal of things brewing inside."

"I think you can over analyze these things", the Aussie said.

"But you are psychologist. You can correct any problems. Am I right?" the boy asked.

"You can only provide the insights and the support for change. Some people can change. Others can't or won't."

The Aussie put his arms around us both and said, "Better to get the right one from the start mates."

My companions helped the hours pass. By the morning I heard Russian over the loud speaker stating that our plane to Saint Petersburg was ready. Soon I would see Alla again.

Alla anxiously waited in the Saint Petersburg airport for me for over six hours. She took me to my hotel room. She drew my bath and put candles and incense around the tub. Alla was like a geisha. She put me to bed. After seeing that I was cared for, she said, "Now sleep, my Swan. Recover your energies. I will return soon."

"Where are you going Alla?"

"I must sleep in my own bed. I never sleep well unless I am in my own bed. I have many such strange things about me, my love. You will in time, learn them all."

"Please, Alla, come sleep with me. Start now to make the habit of my arms being your security, not your bed. We will be married soon. Start getting used to it now."

"You are right." Alla called her mother to tell her that she was staying with me. Alla and her mother were frequently checking with each other on the phone.

Alla curled up next to me. I didn't want to give up the magic of the moment, but I soon fell asleep. Alla couldn't.

Christmas dinner with Alla's parents was different from our first dinner. The food was still abundant and delicious, but this time I was treated as family. Alla had told me not to bring her jewelry for Christmas, as I had planned.

"I am a stylist. I am very fussy about what I wear. Often I prefer to wear inexpensive jewelry, but with a certain color or effect. Just bring some symbolic gifts."

I gave Alla a wallet. Inside the wallet was a credit card. "This is for your airfare to New York and anything you will need for your trip to America." I also gave her bridal magazines, with a card that read, "Pick out some ideas for our wedding". I gave her a silver key ring with the keys to the house and cars. Alla was thrilled.

Alla had gifts for my children and me. Alla's parents and I exchanged gifts as well.

On the morning of December 26, I met my illustrious psychologist and psychiatrist hosts and my interpreter. Alla in her grand style had convinced everyone that I was the most famous psychologist in America. I was shocked that the audience at the medical college was filled with about 250 to 300 psychologists, psychiatrists, and students.

I love to lecture and I spent the next three hours with my

audience. I expected to talk for two hours, but I forgot that the translation would take extra time.

Under Communism, a basic virtue was the idealization of the group above the individual. Now, I was lecturing about becoming more of an individual as a distinction of maturity. Rather than lecturing on the love of the group, I spoke about romantic love. Romantic love is a rebellion from the group.

Alla sat with her best friends, Julia and Tanya, in the front row. They all sat, grinning at me while I spoke.

(If you are not interested in theory, you may skip this section.)

"The pain and frustration of a conflicted relationship, or the demise of a love relationship, are often the reasons many people seek psychological help. Many therapists simply function as a good friend, helping to restore the patient's diminished self-esteem. Often, when patients feel better, they leave treatment and repeat their pattern of disturbed love relationships. Some patients, who are insightful, may stay in psychotherapy and work deep enough to achieve more satisfying love relationships.

Passion has been depicted in poetry, plays, art, novels and music. Only recently has it become a proper study for scientists. The artist can best convey passion, but the scientist can better explain it. Does an analysis kill the appreciation of passion? No more than knowing about art kills the appreciation of art. I believe that the more people understand themselves and the psychology of passion, the better they can love.

I have not found a single theory to adequately explain the complexity of love relations. I have developed my own integrated meta-theory to help understand why romantic love is so irrational. Imagine a pyramid with Species Traits, Individual Traits, Relational Internalizations, Beliefs and Context as five levels. I went to the white board and drew my newly formulated theory (see figure 2).

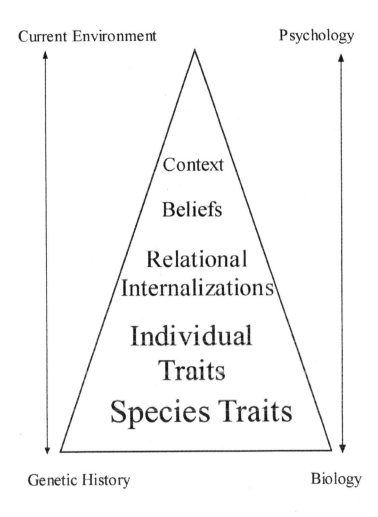

Figure 2: An Integrated Model of Factors Contributing to Love Relations

At the base are the Species Traits we possess as a result of natural selection. What we as a species find attractive in a mate is based on reproductive value. These are concrete and primitive triggers of passion. They were to help the species survive as a whole but have little to do with the survival of a couple's love. The next level is Individual Traits or Temperament. Individuals with a Borderline Personality structure will for example over-idealize and then devalue the love object based on their own affect fluctuations and primitive defenses. Next is the influence of Relational Internalizations from infant attachment and later family dynamics. A secure attachment to a good enough mothering figure and parents who help a child deal with aggression and sexuality are interpersonal prerequisites to loving maturely. The next level is the Beliefs from cultural norms and personal romantic experiences. These beliefs are often superstitious and biased. The top level is the Current Psychological Context. The time in a person's life or current stressful circumstances (ex. Stockholm Syndrome) can produce conditions for an over-idealization of another.

As you move up the pyramid you are moving from Evolutionary History to Current Psychological Context. Each level influences the others. For example, Context eventually will affect natural selection and childhood relations and cultural beliefs can modify instinctual species urges. All these levels in various combinations contribute to the irrationality of romantic love. The most disturbed relationships are based more on: the instinctual concrete reasons for attraction, a Borderline or Psychotic personality structure, toxic internalizations and attachment traumas, irrational beliefs about love objects and a current stressful context that distorts the value of another...

(I gave case examples of each level in more detail. At this point I began to focus on the issues of Temperament. The combination of Temperament issues and traumatic Relational Internalizations produce Personality Disorders.)

Many therapists try to reduce the symptoms of poor relationships by focusing on communication skills. We all can be less defensive and better listeners, but I believe that the main problems with relationships are the result of personality disorders and childhood traumas.

I will now discuss Personality Disorders. Personality Disorders are so much a part of a person's identity that they are ego-syntonic (hardly perceived by the person). Patients may complain of ego-alien symptoms (symptoms that are perceived), such as anxiety and depression, but one's personality is not felt as a symptom. An ego-alien symptom is like a splinter. It doesn't belong and it hurts. An ego-syntonic symptom is like skin. You don't notice it. It's so much a part of you. People with a Personality Disorder tend not to realize that they are defensive, egocentric, provoking conflicts and distorting others.

A Personality Disorder is an enduring pattern of thoughts, feelings and behaviors that are rather inflexible and pervasive. These dysfunctional personality traits cause significant problems in relationships. They often involve frequent mood problems, misinterpretations of others and problems with reasoning and judgment. I will focus on two common Personality Disorders: Narcissistic Personality Disorder and Borderline Personality Disorder. They are specific disorders from a Borderline Personality structure. These common disorders often cause serious interpersonal problems.

A person may have some or all the traits of a Personality Disorder. Many people have parts of different Personality Disorders or one Personality Disorder and features of another (for example, Borderline Personality Disorder with Narcissistic features.) Some people have only some of the symptoms of a Personality Disorder and can be high functioning. Others may have such severe symptoms that they are disabled.

Egocentricity characterizes the Narcissistic Personality Disorder. The person may have grandiosity and act haughty and arrogant. They often have feelings of being special, only understandable to special privileged people. They often have a need for excessive admiration and have a sense of entitlement, in that they expect special treatment from others. However, they often feel infringed upon when similar demands are placed on them. They are often exploitive, have problems with empathy and are unable or unwilling to recognize the feelings and needs of others. They often feel envy and accuse others of envying them. People with a Narcissistic Personality Disorder are often overly concerned with power, success, beauty, or ideal love.

Intense emotions and tumultuous relationships characterize the Borderline Personality Disorder. The person with a Borderline Personality Disorder typically has a history of unstable interpersonal relationships that alternate between idealization and devaluation. One moment they can't live without their love object and the next moment the love object is demonized, persecutory or devalued. They suffer from an unstable self-image. They often do not really feel that they have a distinct identity and they suffer from low self-esteem. They are often impulsive, use bad judgment and are often in a state of confusion. Depression is frequently a problem and may include suicidal thoughts and/or behaviors. There is emotional instability and moodiness, with periods of intense anxiety, agitation and irritability. They frequently have feelings of inner emptiness. They have inappropriate intense anger and can have paranoid thoughts.

If a person's identity is unstable, then that person's perceptions of others will be unstable. The person will love only parts of the love object that excite him or her and will not be able to understand or perceive the whole person.

Let me further discuss the effects of Personality Disorders on love relations. There is some degree of idealization in all love relationships. The more immature the personality, the more intense, subjective and fragile are the idealized love relationships. An immature person's idealization of the loved one is based on both a projected grandiose self and the image of the idealized parent from early childhood.

Many of my ideas come from Otto Kernberg's work on personality structure and love relations (1974, 1975, 1976, 1980,

1985, 1992, 1995, 2002, 2004). Kernberg describes three levels of idealization based on three groupings of personality structure: primitive, neurotic, and normal.

At the primitive level of personality structure, idealization is based on splitting. Splitting occurs when people see themselves and others as either all good or all bad. They have difficulty emotionally accepting the complex nature of people and relate to others in terms of their needs and projections. The other person is perceived as good, if they believe that person might meet their needs. The other person is perceived as bad or useless, if the person does not meet their needs.

At this primitive level, a person falls in love with a part object, not a whole person. The object of desire represents erotic and dependent needs. There is a great deal of idealization without empathy for the beloved.

A man might feel passion for a woman because of what she symbolizes and evokes. This might be his frustrating and teasing mother. She might see him as both the protective mother and the idealized father. However, they are in love with representations from the unconscious, which are parts of the self and parts of the child's perceptions of the parents. All this combines to a fantasy of an erotic image. Borderline and Narcissistic personalities can quickly move from intense idealization to devaluation. They fall in love with projections of their grandiose self and idealized parental images. However, since they have problems with impulse control and aggression, the intimacy is often destroyed. This idealization is fragile.

If a person is not mature, the destructive aspects of passion dominate the intimacy. Sexuality can become intense, dominated by aggression and emotional sado-masochism.

All passion requires some sado-masochism. The word, "passion" originally meant "to suffer", as in "The Passion of Jesus". Passionate love is primitive and aggressive. Immature individuals can be very passionate, but they end up letting their aggression or need to suffer destroy the relationship. Healthier individuals are able to keep the sado-masochism in the playful and teasing aspects of the eroticism without harm to the relationship.

People with Borderline and Narcissistic Personality Disorders unconsciously wish that ideal love and sexual gratification from the new love object would overcome their inner conflicts. While Borderline Personalities seek a dependent relationship and resent the person they depend on, the Narcissistic person fears dependency. Narcissistic Personalities defensively cover up their dependency needs with self-righteous demands and feelings of entitlement.

Both Borderline and Narcissistic Personalities may fear imprisonment in intimacy, since they project their own need to exploit and control onto the love object. They project the denied worst parts of themselves onto the partner. They also tend to act out in order to provoke the partner to react as the persecutory object. That way, they can assure themselves that they now have the power to escape from and punish the love object.

Borderline Personalities fear separation from sources of security. Separations can lead to decomposition. Devaluing the object of dependency is a common defense. When faced with separation, criticism, or frustration, they project the impaired self onto the partner and go into a rage.

At first, Narcissistic and Borderline Personalities may be difficult to detect due to their warmth, charm, and talent. However, their inner emptiness, dissatisfaction, and rage soon become evident, when they feel they are not getting what they want.

They tend to experience the ordinary reciprocity of human relations as exploitive and unfair. The partner must become exactly as they need him or her to be. They regard any limits as rejection.

Their partner needs emotional masochism and denial in order to remain a self-object to the Narcissistic and Borderline lover. In time, however, the Borderline and Narcissistic lover will use up the self-object lover and will either provoke the lover to reject them or devalue the lover and leave.

The second level is the Neurotic Personality structure. The idealization found with individuals with Neurotic Personalities is more reality based than with the primitive level. The image of the idealized parent is transferred to the new love object to form the basis for love and conflict. Rather than problems with denial, reality distortion and aggression that characterize the first level, the main problems at this level are inhibition, anxiety and guilt.

A person with a Neurotic Personality structure has the capacity for empathy and awareness of the whole love object. At this level, there is remorse and concern, because the conscience is well developed. However, neurosis comes with too strong a superego (conscience), so there is often sexual inhibition and guilt that compromises the intimacy.

Often, people with a Neurotic Personality structure and a Narcissistic/Borderline Personality structure fall in love. They are complementary relationships. The Neurotic Personality has empathy, guilt and masochism to put up with the exploitive, aggressive personality. They are gratified vicariously by the Narcissistic/Borderline person's expression of sexuality and aggression without neurotic guilt. On the other hand, the Narcissistic/Borderline person sees the Neurotic Personality as containing and anchoring them. This alliance is often filled with conflict and instability.

Finally, normal idealization in love is based on a stable identity and realistic awareness and appreciation of the whole love object. The mature person has the capacity to remain in love, since the love is based on a complex perception of the other's qualities that involve abstractions such as ideals, values, and goals. The idealization is based less on overcompensations, projections, and transferences, and more on the reality of the person. There is erotic desire for the other with little guilt to interfere with sexuality and intimacy. There is an ability to identify with the other's gender. There is a high capacity for empathy, tolerance, insight, remorse, and tenderness. There is a healthy concern for the other and few problems with aggression and defensiveness."

At the end of my lecture, I took questions from the audience. One young psychiatry student wondered, "Dr. Gordon, it would seem that, according to what you are saying, there is little hope for the average person to remain happily married."

I laughed along with everyone and said, "It is hard to remain happily married. There are many internal and external pressures working against it. No one is entitled to a lasting love without work. If we put as much work into our intimacies as we do in other things, the intimacies may stay in better condition. Marriage involves work; however, if it is frequent, hard work, then something is wrong, and a major change in personality or a more suitable partner may be required. Deep psychotherapy may be needed for such changes, but not necessarily. I have seen people with Personality Disorders happily married. They keep the hostility and defensiveness to a minimum and give each other a lot of psychological room. There needs to be insight and self-knowledge to reduce acting out internal conflicts. When there is acting out, then there needs to be remorse and responsibility for one's actions. When the beloved regresses, there needs to be forgiveness. The couple needs to express an appreciation and support for one another. The most important thing is to marry someone who you not only want to be with, but also is easy enough to be with. But sometimes things work out simply because the rocks in his head perfectly fit the holes in her head!"

Chapter 27

Irina's Warning

Alla was beaming when she came up to me after my lecture. "Tanya and Julia said that you are a great guru and that I need to become rich and support you, so that you will be free to do your thinking and writing. They also said that you were describing me, but I told them that what you were saying was true of all people." Alla proudly hung on me, as we thanked everyone. I was her prize, her guru.

During this visit, I often saw Alla's quick temper and impatience. Alla hated the winter in Saint Petersburg. She had told me that it was a time of deep depression for her. She could not tolerate the cold dark days with little sun. People who experience Seasonal Affective Disorder may also have underlying problems with depression and the two add up to a more acute depressive reaction (Murray, Hay, & Armstrong, 1995).

Alla was in a bad mood after fighting with her boss. She came to my hotel room in a rage. "That bastard called me in to question my expense account! How dare he!"

It made me think of our fight over money. I listened to Alla rant and rave. Alla's body shook with rage. I wondered how often she would be like that with me. People often think that they will be the exception to the rule. I was seeing problems in Alla, but I loved her. I decided that I would be patient with her.

Besides, she soon slowly undressed. As I watched her, I

took a mental photograph of her. I told myself to remember this visual moment of erotic beauty. That mental photo is still clear in my mind. Now, I think that I was at some level concerned that it might not last and I wanted to save this moment in my memory. Alla then wrapped herself around me and I was soon lost in her charms.

I caught a cold I think from the long chilly wait at the airport. Alla's mother insisted that I move in with them, so they could care for me. I slept in Alla's room. Alla slept with her mother and her father slept on the sofa. This arrangement said a lot about the family system. Alla was not the one on the sofa but in a symbiotic union with her mother.

For over a week, we lived together in her home. Alla loved caring for me. She put mustard paste on my chest. She swore by this cure. She loved to feed me and hold me. I was in Alla's room, vulnerable and totally under her control. It was a love that she understood.

As we laid in bed, I asked Alla, "Honey, are you preparing for your move to the U.S.?"

"No. I have too many things to do. Really, Darling, I have no time to even think of it! Please can we speak of other things?"

Later Alla said, "Darling, you were so great with your lecture, I am certain that you could become famous here and have a practice in Saint Petersburg."

"Alla, I can live wherever the money is, but it is very unlikely that I can have the standard of living in Russia with psychology that I now have in the United States."

"Then, Darling, you can have a practice in both places. I'm sure you can do it. We can buy a condo here and fly back and forth each month." Alla was telling me that she was terrified to go too far from her ego-defining status in Saint Petersburg.

Alla's mother invited another interpreter into her home and the three of us went into the living room. Irina closed the doors. Alla stayed in her room.

Irina began, "After Alla showed us your funny, lovely e-mail that you wrote to my husband and me, I wrote you a long letter about Alla's problems. I tried to get her to send it to you, but she never did. I will tell you now, what I said in my letter.

Robert, you were wrong to say, 'Fuck you' to Alla. She was crying hysterically, and had even for a while removed your photos from her wall. She never had a man's photos on her walls. She was never really in love before. I must tell you how to handle Alla. It will not be easy. She cannot handle any confrontation—that is the wrong way. Alla has a bad temper and terrible moods, as did her father. She can be very cruel to me and say the most awful things to hurt me. But the next day, she remembers nothing. I will be upset all week and she is hugging and kissing me as though nothing happened. She won't even apologize. Only recently, since you appeared in her life, does she sometimes apologize. Do not confront her. Do not use your psychology. It will not help and may make things worse. I know. I have tried. She doesn't remember what she says in her terrible moods. Just use that nice smile of yours, wait and it will pass.

It is better to talk her into things. She is very suggestible. You love her sincerely, I know, but you need to understand her better. She is a very talented girl, but do not be fooled, she is really very weak.

I know you are worried about the age difference. Don't worry about it. That will not be the problem. She will be loyal to you. She loves you completely. I know my daughter. This is the first time she has ever been this much in love. She loved that the men loved her so much. The main problem will be handling her terrible moods.

Don't talk of marriage. She is terrified of marriage. After she came back from Finland, she was very depressed about that relationship. She saw Nadya. Nadya hypnotized her. Alla told me that she remembered as a child, being in a carriage. Her father was drinking, and he left the carriage unattended. The carriage went down a hill. Alla remembers screaming. I didn't know about that event, but I did have to leave that marriage because I was frightened for Alla's safety. She gets close to marriage and then she leaves. So please don't talk of marriage. Live together for a while. Let her get used to it. Do you understand?"

"Da."

"Did you notice that when you give Alla money, she gives it to me? She knows that she is impulsive and cannot save. She does not understand limits. We fight about money all the time. At some level, she must know, because she still lets me manage the money. Be prepared; she will be very angry at your limits, but she needs them. In the next moment, it's as if the fight never happened.

My daughter loves you completely, but, please, you will need a great deal of patience with her. You will need to understand and survive her terrible moods and forget the things that she says in them. That is the only way this can work out.

Oh, I'm afraid that I am doing all the talking. Do you understand? Do you have any questions?"

"No not at all. Thank you for your honest and helpful advice."

Irina was very brave to share this with me. She was a proud and private person. I was sure that it was hard for her, especially in front of an interpreter. Irina wanted me to be able to help her daughter. I think that she saw that possibility. She saw that Alla was now able to apologize. Perhaps Irina feared that I might not tolerate her daughter's problems. She wanted me to know how to possibly make it work.

This time I did not think that Irina was trying to chase me away. I did not fully appreciate everything that Irina said, but I stored everything. I thanked Irina for her help and went to join Alla in her room.

Alla offered me some cognac and asked me if our talk went well. I said, "Your mother gave me an Alla manual, so I can better understand you."

Alla laughed and said, "It won't help. Only a large stock of time and love will help to understand this unique creature." Alla began to kiss me and seduce me away from any concerns.

The next day we joined Alla's friends, Julia and Tanya, at Alla's favorite café. Julia asked Alla something and Alla snapped, "Fuck You!" Julia looked hurt.

I asked, "Alla, what did Julia say?"

"She asked if we had a wedding date."

"Why would you say 'fuck you' to that?"

Alla just shrugged and changed the subject. It was as if it never happened.

We visited a famous psychiatrist who had helped to host my lecture. He gave us a tour around his clinic and showed us his patients getting intravenous anti-psychotic medication in their beds. Alla looked at the patients and became anxious.

"Darling, I must leave this place immediately. I'll meet you outside."

Later I asked Alla what had been the problem.

"Robert, my heart bleeds to see so much suffering."

I did not see sympathy in her. I saw anxiety. I think that the patients represented her mental illness. She ran from them, just the way she ran from the awareness of her own problems.

Christmas is a minor holiday for the Russians, while New Year's Eve is their big holiday. In Alla's living room next to the TV, was a decorated New Year's tree. Again, Alla's mother made a great dinner. At midnight, we watched President Putin on TV wish us all a good New Year. Alla and her parents sang traditional Russian songs. We then watched entertainers on the TV.

There was a comedian talking about Russian women going to the U.S. to get married.

He said, "Their American husbands work all the time. In order to break the loneliness, the Russian brides go to the shopping malls to spend their husband's money. They can't wait to return to Russia. Here they find true happiness again, tormenting their friends by telling them about their good life in America...The girl friend will ask, 'How many rooms has your house in America?' 'Well, lets see, the five bed rooms, the study, the living room, the dining room, the kitchen..'. 'Oh, we have the same, only without the walls.'"

Alla was trying to interpret for me in between her fits of laughter. It was a wonderful evening.

When Irina said her goodbye to me, she cried and looked at me with a knowing sadness. At the airport, Alla became very upset. She seemed to panic and wither. When I arrived home, I received the good news that Alla had her interview date for the fiancée visa on February 15th.

Chapter 28

The Confrontation

Karen came early for her session. I opened the door to my waiting room and Karen smiled when she saw me. She came into the session, put her check on my desk and laid on the couch. She was quiet for a while and then spoke with a tremor.

"My mom flipped out on me and smacked me across my face. She told me that you are ruining our relationship." Karen reached for the tissue box and wiped her tears.

"Why did she hit you?"

"She can really go into rages. First I told her that I would be coming over for dinner at 4:30 on Friday's and not at 3:30. She wasn't happy about that. Then I told her that I wanted to know why they got a divorce. She told me 'some things are the worse for the dwelling'. Then she changed the subject. I wasn't buying it this time. She took off on you, calling you a quack and a rapist. But I persisted. Finally she told me that it was because my father molested me."

Karen was pressing her hands against her head as if she needed to keep her mind from exploding.

"I said, 'Mom that was after you and him separated, what's the real reason'? Then she said, 'your father was running around. When I caught him he tried to kill me. He tried to poison me. He had me put in the loony bin. Those quack psychiatrists believed him. He was going to use that to take you away from me.'"

"I take it your mother doesn't think she has any problems," I said.

"Mom thinks that she is fine. Her house is a mess. She can't tell what is important and what isn't. She can't throw anything away. Her house is scary. She can't hold a job. She has no close friends. She told me that she wouldn't date so she could devote herself to me. That's bullshit. She can't get along."

"Karen, what evidence did she have that your father was having affairs?"

"She told me that she smelled vaginal juices on father."

"That was her evidence?"

"I told her that it was not possible. She started screaming at me; screaming that men were evil; that my father had affairs and tried to poison her. That he spread rumors about her so that no one would hire her. That he paid off the psychiatrists to say that she was crazy. That he molested me."

"What were you feeling?"

"I was upset, but I needed to know. I asked her how she knew that I was molested. She told me that all the doctors agreed that I was. I kept asking how she knew. She said that I had a sex rash on my vagina. I said, 'Mom what the hell is a sex rash? I had rashes there all the time. All girls get them. It doesn't mean that they were molested! I never remembered Dad molesting me! I wanted to make you happy mom, so I just went along with it. Then I became confused.' She slapped me and told me to leave. She told me that you were brainwashing me and that she was reporting you to the licensing board."

"I'm not worried. How are you? I am worried about you."

"Dr. Gordon, I feel like everything I ever thought was bullshit. I feel like my core is hollow, fake. I feel so alone. I think that she is paranoid. I always felt that but I never really put it all together and accepted it. She was my rock. Now I feel afloat. I don't know who to rely on now."

"Karen, you have to lose the idealized image of your mother

to find out who you are. Now you will need to rely on your own weighing of evidence as you deal with reality."

"I'm going to contact my aunt Michelle and see what I can learn about my father."

Chapter 29

The Mutual Expectation Stage

In the Mutual Expectation Stage the lovers try to meet each other's expectations of a committed relationship. If practical problems around economic, emotional, social and sexual issues are not resolved the relationship will weaken or end.

Jan. 13

In a month, Alla would be in Moscow at the U.S. consulate for her interview. About two weeks after that, she would be in America. I was preparing for her arrival and our marriage.

"Alla, if you want your parents at the wedding, you need to work on getting their visas."

"Don't talk about marriage! No more talk of it, Robert, please!"

"What's wrong?"

"I...I...can't deal with all this...I...I..."

"If you need more time, there is no rush. Don't feel pressured. If the 90 days in America is not enough time for you to be sure about marriage, we can just go through the visa application process again."

"Robert, you were married. I never was. How can you do that? I can't imagine looking at the same face every day for years. I am too wild for marriage! I am used to being independent. I can't stand to be dependent and trapped. I am not sure I can do that."

"O.K. Don't worry. We can put things off."

Alla sounded angry, scared and drunk. This was not the usual anxiety about marriage. Alla made an issue of independence because her own dependency needs scared her. She projected her dependency needs onto me. She feared that I would want to control her the same way she needed to control me. This made marriage a trap in Alla's mind. Irina's warning came back to me. I was no exception.

Jan. 14
"Alla, I have stopped all my wedding plans—no plans, just time for us to learn more about each other. Please do not feel forced or pressured. Be as nervous as anyone should be when about to leap to the next dimension. But you are leaping to an adventure, not your death! Turn your 'Oh Shit!'" into an 'Oh Wow!'"

"Thank you for the kind words. My weariness from the filming of the fashion show and PMS were the only reason for my pessimistic words."

"Alla, your country, your room, and your familiar things can only give the illusion of security. You know that only by challenging yourself can you keep developing a portable inner security."

"Yes, I need to leave Russia. No doubt. I need to see the next dimension. I need to find a portable inner security. I need you!"

I hoped that Alla would show insight about her fears. Otherwise, she might find an unconscious solution, such as provoking a fight as a way to back out of our relationship. In the past Alla told me what I wanted to hear. Now I needed to hear real insight and concern before I could go on.

Jan. 16

"Saint Petersburg irritates me now...I had a very unpleasant conversation with my boss at the filming. Then I was warring with my mum. I hate the world when you are far."

"You really sounded scared of marriage."

"I have no fears about marriage. I never had marriage before. I just don't understand it. I got used to being free. I got used to not promising stability. I am too wild for boring stability."

Alla saw her being too wild as a virtue and not a flaw. What Alla called "wild" was in fact her narcissism and aggression. Rationalizing a flaw keeps it alive and destructive.

Jan. 17

"Alla, independence and freedom come from a secure identity. Fear of dependency in a relationship is usually a result of fearing one's own dependency needs. You are too wild for boring stability? You couple "boring" with "stability." I am stable and interesting. Someone can be an unstable bore. Very emotional people often see an emotionally healthy relationship as boring.

Boredom can be about an inner loneliness and discontent. In a loving, committed relationship, you feel contentment that is not dramatic or showy."

"My Gentle Vulture why are you so pessimistic?"

"Because of what you said."

"What did I say?"

"Alla, you said, 'don't talk about marriage! I can't imagine looking at the same face every day for years...I am too wild for marriage...I am used to being independent...I am not sure I can do that.' Don't you remember?"

"I said that! No I don't remember."

"How is it possible that you can't remember something so important?"

"Sorry, Robert, I can't give a long explanation now, because I must now try to make a list of the most important things for my future long trip to you. I promised my boss that I would finish my spring collection before I left...I have received an offer to work for a French designer in Paris!"

Alla forgot what she said and hoped that I would as well. Alla showed no concern about my feelings. Her 'To Do' list included both leaving for America and also looking into a possible job in Paris. It was provocative. Alla was dropping emotional land mines all over our conversation.

Jan. 18

"Robert, I said that I couldn't look at the same face for years? I said that? Don't remember. I swear! O, God...I saw your face for 3000 years, and I am still alive, by the way. And I need more."

"Alla, you put me on an emotional roller coaster and you don't seem to realize it."

"Yes, I didn't realize this."

"You really didn't consider how I would feel?"

"I remember saying to you some words, but I was meaning, 'Let's don't talk about it right now! Not right now!' Because when I have a bad mood, PMS, headache, or other terrible stupid pessimistic ideas in my head, I don't want to talk at all... This is because all my words can be only bullshit from a baby, who is just afraid...I remember about my previous unpleasant dialogue with you by phone, when I tried to speak during my bad state of health or bad mood...As when I did not understand you when we spoke about money."

"Alla, your 'only bullshit from a baby' is upsetting. When do you take responsibility for your words and their consequences?"

"I can hurt you accidentally! I knew that I was upset on the phone and I tried to protect you from this heavy mood. That is why I said: 'Let's don't talk about marriage.' I was meaning 'Honey, I don't want to tell you any stupid words right now'. Now, you understand me better, my Swan? I need time for myself. I need only your words about love. I am coming to love you and care about you, honey...It's my way. It's my plan...I need to have happy marriage with you."

"So when you say your bullshit from a baby, what do I do? Do I go into denial as well?"

"Do not be the psychologist with me. Do not try to give me a diagnosis; just give me time, without questions and explanations. I will struggle with my demons independently. I do not want to disturb you and hurt you...Give me time...Even stay away from me, honey during my inner war."

"Don't use my being a psychologist as the problem. Anyone would want to understand what is going on. You don't get to make unilateral decisions on when a topic is open or closed."

"You will need to live with me for understanding...If we shall have the decision to get married on the second day after my arrival to your home, we are crazy twins, it's possible!.. If we shall have the desire, we'll get married without my parents...OK, my Love?.. Nothing can stop us...Don't worry...We'll find a way, relax...Just love me, nothing more. I just need you!.. What do you think, nice idea?.. Come to me, closer, my Gentle Vulture, you drive me crazy."

"I thought you are too wild for marriage."

"Don't worry about my phrase. I will keep my wildness close to you. Please use it and enjoy it...Oh, I used my credit card in Frankfurt...Honey, it so is convenient. Thank you. It felt great with your magic gift. I have bought good cosmetics, gifts for parents, for you and a few new shoes, shoes all the time, it's a women's fetish; you don't mind, my patron do you?

...I spent not too much. Only you can to defuse this cute 'bomb', Honey, only you. I need you. Just love me...I shall not give any explanations...I will not apologize for my nature. It's all about me!!...I can be dangerous to all people on this planet... except for you...I sent some funny pictures for you honey...You are my soul mate and I love you madly! Just be close to me, love me, use me for your pleasure, and be happy."

Alla saw insight, which she called "psychology," as dangerous. She was not prepared to look deeply into herself. If she looked too deep she would have to give up her defensive mythology that sustained her. She was play acting her life and she never had a fairy tale childhood. She was not strong enough to deal with the loss of her father and that part of her that was similar to her father.

The pictures that Alla sent were both seductive and disturbing. In one photo, she was dressed provocatively in a negligee, looking sad and holding a knife to her head. The photos were a warning of her self-destructiveness.

Alla provoked conflict and then denied it. She could not apologize nor understand how her actions affected another.

When Alla said, "I can be dangerous for all people on this planet, except for you," I knew that meant that I was next. I was not the exception. No one ever is.

Jan. 19

"Alla, no one is entitled to being loved regardless of how they act. There needs to be insight, responsibility and remorse to help keep love alive. You are too complacent about your emotional dumping. It has a cumulative effect on relationships. Please take responsibility for your words. Don't expect others to have to put up with it. Babies, when they feel upset, just vomit on their parents. Parents just wipe it up and love the baby. Adults don't have such expectations in their relationships."

"Robert, you think that I am not mature enough for marriage! We had only a few of unpleasant conversations, and you are already in a panic!...Why do you sound like an offended baby? I am not your mother!!...You attempt to justify your own problems and you want that I pay for them! You can't be just a loving person...You suspect that I don't know what healthy love is...You tell me 'Alla this is not about love but sickness...'"

"So what looked like an insight was really an unshared resentment waiting to be used. You now bring this up as a complaint about me as though I gave you an unfair criticism. One slashed his veins for you and another rejected his child so not to disturb you. Alla, you offered these as demonstrations of real love. Now you are offended that I said this was sick? Do you expect me also to love you the same way? I will not give you such a 'love.' I would never accept such a 'love.'

Love is not unconditional tolerance. That is masochism. Love is showing concern and remorse if you hurt someone close to you. Love is taking feedback that you were wrong and wanting to be a better person."

"Robert, I am tired to apologize for my temper!!.... I don't want a war.

I am too sensitive and gentle for this terrible way.

I did nothing that needs apology. Honey, you do not love my nature. I see it...You want to make me a stable quiet woman, mature for the long relations in the suburbia USA...I will not allow you to use me as rabbit for your experiments and proof of your theories. After your psychology I became worse...I want to stop it! Now!"

Alla was in a rage. I was not mirroring back her grandiose self-image. She needed me to tolerate all her problems and defenses. Otherwise, I would become devalued and an ice statue to her.

I was still in conflict about ending it. I was still hoping, beyond reason, that Alla would have insight. I kept holding on to the magical times I had with her. These periodic rages seemed like visits from another being. A relationship builds over time and dies over time. Denial has a hand in both periods.

Jan. 24

"Alla I missed you."

"I missed you my Swan. I could not eat or sleep all these days without you. I have no life without you."

"I want to clarify my concern. Honey, I remember a couple that saw me a while back. The wife said, 'I am leaving him. He doesn't understand me. He is always a physician. I was mortified. We were making love and he began to give me an examination! That was the last straw!' The husband tearfully said, 'I was about to make love to her and I was fondling her breasts when I felt a lump. It seemed attached. I do this sort of work. It needs a biopsy as soon as possible. I know she is scared. I know she would rather fight with me than face that something may be wrong with her. Usually, I just let her get angry with me and it blows over, but I can't ignore this one. I love her, and I am concerned for her.'

I only saw them one session. They never came back. I don't know what happened, but I've been in his shoes.

To say nothing about a loved one's self-destructiveness is moral negligence. That is different from unfair criticism. Alla, I tell people things no one has ever said to them before, things they don't know about themselves, things people would swear are absolutely untrue about them. These diagnoses are about an unconscious side of personality.

Do you think when I diagnose people with a Narcissistic Personality Disorder that they realize they have it? These personality traits are their normal, their skin. They do not perceive these self-defeating traits as personal problems, but they affect them and their relationships. They seem like they have very high self-esteem, but it is overcompensation for their inferiority complexes. They become overly dependent on the admiration of others to help regulate their vulnerable self-esteem. They cannot stand criticism.

They think I'm full of shit, if I suggest such a thing to them. They only come to me because of long-standing problems with intimacy that they think are the result of others. I go through the traits of Narcissism with them:
-Needs to see self as special
-Preoccupied with thoughts of beauty, and/or ideal love
-Requires excessive admiration
-Has sense of entitlement
-Impatient
-Tends to be unaware of empathic failures to others

Or I describe Borderline Personality traits such as:
-Intense intimate relationships alternating between the extremes of idealization and devaluation
-Identity instability
-Impulsiveness

-Emotional instability, depression, irritability lasting a few hours or a few days

-Periods of feelings of emptiness

-Periods of inappropriate, intense anger

-Dissociated memory or denials after periods of upset

Some people have a few of these traits, while others have most of them.

I then give examples of each of the criteria in their own lives, so they can see how they apply. They often ask what can be done.

I tell them, 'If you do not have insight, you will go through life blaming everyone else for your unhappiness and never have a lasting satisfying intimacy. With psychotherapy, I might be able to help you.'

Alla please reread our emails. We can all learn from looking back with insight. Sometimes we need the help of a professional to achieve personal growth. Alla go to a good psychotherapist and learn to be less self-defeating. I tell you this out of loving concern."

"Robert, thank you for your wise words."

I felt an obligation before I left to tell Alla that she was suffering from problems that required professional care. Alla felt that anytime I took issue with her behavior that I was unjustly diagnosing her. In the end, I did give Alla a diagnosis. I did it with concern. I felt that although our relationship was lost, at least I might plant some seeds that might later be useful.

Jan. 25

"Robert, I know everything already, even my Narcissistic Personality and other stuff! Do you think that I am stupid? You might have a better knowledge but not a better mind...I agree with that doctor's wife who said: 'We were making love and he begins to give me an examination! That was the last straw!'...I am on her side...Are you afraid that my Narcissistic Personality Disorder will disturb your ego?"

"Alla, I cannot live on an emotional roller coaster with someone who even denies the roller coaster. There is no hope with your denial. Please, it is better for both of us to end it now. It will spare us worse pain later."

"My intuition was right! You lied to me all along! No one finishes so terribly a rare relation like this. Normal people do other more healthy things...You just decided to leave me earlier, than I leave you! HA! So petty a way!...I do not respect you for it!...I had a premonition that you will do a huge mistake that you will regret. I prepared for it...You are forbidden to disturb me again!...You no longer exist for me. I never look back...I do not need to check our past e-mails for understanding. I am destroying them all. I trust my intuition more...

I am glad for this...I am fortunate to be free of such an old sick man as you...I would have died from boredom close to you after a few weeks...Leave your dreams, Robert. Open your eyes, finally! I loved not you. I loved my fantasy. I loved an illusion."

I was Alla's illusion. She fell in love with her over-idealized image of me that represented her need for a transformational magical love. When I insisted on a reciprocal intimacy, her idealization switched over to total devaluation. Alla could not perceive me as existing somewhere in reality between the extremes of her personality. Some degree of idealization and even devaluation occurs in all intimacy. They hopefully are part of a normal ambivalent love that is based on real qualities and shared values. But for individuals with an immature personality structure, the idealization and devaluation becomes so extreme that they determine the course of the relationship.

Alla was caught between her fear of a real intimacy and losing me. She was caught between living within her fragile fantasy world, where she was the child-queen and the adult reality world of give and take. If she had insight, she might have grown over time. Denial was her tragic flaw.

Alla's problems were relationship killers. I could have followed Irina's advice. But I would be managing the relationship. I wanted a mutually satisfying intimacy.

Alla had to deal with the pain of rejection and loss. This was Alla's deepest love and its failure was traumatic and humiliating for her. She sought in me the mentally ill father to save and the hero father to save her. She hoped to repair her past and herself through an idealized magical love with me.

It was hard for Alla to go forward. She distrusted men and she feared separation from her mother. She never developed an inner sense of security. Commitment and long distances from a secure base frightened her. Alla did not develop a secure portable identity. Since Alla feared looking at her past and herself, she would repeat her love drama. I started as her idealized father and ended up her devalued lost father. I also went from being her grandiose twin to becoming the embodiment of her damaged self.

Ironically, I helped Karen and many people like her with empathy and insight. Alla's mood disorder, Personality Disorder and childhood traumas were treatable. The tragedy of Alla was that she was too defensive.

Alla never wanted to review our correspondences as a check on reality. Alla did not think she ever got reality wrong. She only needed her intuition as her guide. Alla never saw the contradictions in her intuition. Her intuition told her we were meant to be together. Later her intuition told her I was unworthy of her love. That did not matter. All that mattered was Alla would live in a world of her own making where she was a self-imposed prisoner. In the end, she agreed with the wife of the physician in my example. Alla identified with the defensive wife who would rather be alone and possibly die than look at herself. Alla projected her mental illness onto me. I became the devalued ice statue.

All Alla's problems were clear from her first charming and grandiose letters to me, to her first signs of rage and devaluation. Everything was evident from the start.

At first, my conscious knowledge of psychology did not protect me from acting out my unconscious psychology. But in the end I went with my values of a healthy relationship over the excitement of the passion. Passion is powerful. Our passion springs from our instinctual and personal pasts. It remains in the most basic level of our personality. However, my psychology helped me to recognize the problems and kept me from remaining in a disturbed relationship for long. My psychology helped me to tear myself away, even while I felt intense passion for her.

It is a mistake to love someone so much that you are willing to sacrifice your sense of fairness and values. I was wrong to lose site of my wish for a sweet and non-defensive partner.

I grieved for Alla. I missed her. At times, I hoped that she would reread our correspondences and have a miraculous insight cure. My loss was painful, but I also felt relieved. While my mind was trying to avoid the reality of the problems, my body had been absorbing the stress of it. Now, my blood pressure, which had increased, decreased. My shoulder pain, which lasted for months, went away.

Alla would have been a terrible mistake. Thank God for psychology.

Chapter 30

The Breakthrough

Karen's manner of dress was not as provocative and neither were her actions. Karen's voice was less shrill and had more sadness and depth. These changes were mostly unconscious.

"I visited my aunt Michelle. She cried when she saw me. She made me cry. It's been years since I've seen her. I told her about my work with you. She told me that I was brave. She told me that my dad loved mom and me a lot. She said that he tried to get her to go to a psychiatrist, but she refused.

Michelle said that mom was insanely jealous and was always looking for evidence of affairs. Oh and she knew about mom's paranoia about smelling vaginal juices on him and about being poisoned. She said that dad left after she locked me out of her bedroom while she was having a psychotic breakdown. He saw the condition I was in and took me to live with him. He had mom hospitalized.

Michelle said that she was to supervise mom's visits with me after the hospitalization. She said that mom was fighting dad for custody of me, and that's when she accused dad of molesting me. She lost in court. But mom made me afraid to see him. I now remember how she would examine me for evidence of sex abuse after I saw him. Eventually I was telling the therapist that I was abused. Mom taught me that he was evil and I believed her. Finally, I refused to see dad.

My mom wouldn't let Michelle in the house and forbade

me to see her. My aunt said that dad would send checks to me. Mom must have cashed them, but told me that he never sent me money. He also sent me cards and presents. Michelle called once to see if I were getting them. I wasn't. Mom told her that she was protecting me from him. She hung up on my aunt. Michelle didn't call her again until dad died. She said that she would take me to the funeral."

"How old were you?"

"About 15. My mom told me that I didn't have to go. She took me out to a nice restaurant and we celebrated his death."

"Did you ever go to his grave?"

"No. Michelle showed me pictures of dad holding me and playing checkers with me. I remembered that I loved playing checkers with him. He'd let me win and pretend to be angry. I'd climb on his back.

God, I remember the smell of his cologne. I remember his tenderness. I have memories of my dad!...I remember waiting for him to come home...

I remember his love...how he hugged me...I miss him...I loved my daddy...I miss my daddy!"

Karen had a breakthrough. She had the courage to look into her past. She could now understand why she was so afraid to love and would only commit to the sort of men that she could easily reject. Karen's image of a man was affected by her psychotic mother's paranoia. Buried beneath that was the memories of the relationship with her father. Karen needed to understand her mother's problems in order to reevaluate her beliefs about men and intimacy. Karen's feelings about men were mainly due to her mother as her first love object. Karen feared losing her identity to a man, since her mother had invaded and controlled her identity. Karen had an anxious and ambivalent attachment to her mother. This characterized itself in her romantic relationships and in her transference to me.

Eventually Karen used her emotional insights to begin to detoxify her childhood traumas. This understanding in time would lead to a more solid identity and a greater capacity for a healthy intimacy. Karen's memory of a loving protective father can act as a foundation for a better relationship with a man.

Karen still had a long way to go. Karen's breakthrough was an entry point into deeper work with less resistance. Tragically, Karen's insights came too late in life to reunite with her father. But I knew that Karen would be able to love better because of the love he had given her.

I was surprised how these two women turned out. Karen used insight and improved. Alla used denial and remained unhappy. My heart wished for two happy endings.

Epilogue

I began to write this book soon after I ended the relationship with "Alla". I picked the name "Alla" since I felt that it is a beautiful Russian name. Writing was therapeutic. It helped the primitive side of my brain which stores emotional bonding, catch up with the rational side of my brain that knew that it was a bad relationship. I needed to grieve it, learn from it and go on to pick more wisely.

By May of 2002 I was ready to date again. I answered an intriguing personal ad. Now I would not end a book with a coincidence, but this is the truth. She responded with a charming email and signed it with her name...Alla.

She was a beautiful Russian Alla living about an hour from me. She had similar interests and talents as the "Alla" in my book, but with crucial differences in personality—wonderful differences. I was initially attracted to her because of the similarities, but I fell in love with her because of those wonderful differences in maturity.

We had the sort of passion that can blow up an infatuation with its intensity. But we could talk honestly and openly. That kept the passion alive and enduring. We became passionate best friends. In about one year we married. It became a love better than I could have ever imagined. I can now look back and see how I have been affected by all my intimacies. And within intimacy we have the choice to repeat the past or to grow from it.

References

Ainsworth, M. D., Blehar, M., Waters, E., and Wall, S. (1978). *Patterns of Attachment*.: Hillsdale, NJ: Erlbaum.

Akhtar, S. (1999). *Inner Torment—Living Between Conflict and Fragmentation*: Jason Aronson Inc. New Jersey, London.

Arlow. J. (1991). Methodology and reconstruction. *Psychoanalytic Quarterly, 60*, 539-563.

Aron, A. and Aron, E.N. (1989). *The Heart of Social Psychology*.: Lexington, M.A: Lexington Books.

Bemporad, Jules R. and Romano, Steven J. (1993). Childhood experience and adult depression: A review of studies. *Journal of Psychoanalysis, 53*(4), 301-315.

Bergmann, M. (1982). Platonic love, transference love and love in real life. *Journal of the American Psychoanalytic Association.*(30), 87-112.

Bergmann, M. S. (1995). On love and it's enemies. *Psychoanalytic Review*(821), 1-19.

Bion, W. R. (1962a). *Learning from Experience*: London: Heinemann.

Bourdon, K. H. B., J.H.; Rae, D.S. et.al. (1988). Gender differences in phobia: Results of the ECA community survey. *Journal of Anxiety Disorders., 2*(3), 227-241.

Bowlby, J. (1982). *Attachment and loss*: New York: Jason Aronson.

Brown, D., Scheflin, A. W., Whitfield, C. L.,. (1999). Recovered memories: The current weight of the evidence in science and in the courts. *Journal of Psychiatry & Law.*, *27*(1), 5-156.

Browne, M. A., Oakley; J., Wells, J. E., Bushnell, J. A., Hornblow, A. R. (1995). Disruptions in childhood parental care as risk factors for major depression in adult women. *Australian & New Zealand Journal of Psychiatry, 29*(3), 437-448.

Buss, D. M. (1994). *The evolution of desire : strategies of human mating*. New York: BasicBooks.

Dicks, H. V. (1967). *Marital Tensions*: New York: Basic Books.

Eisenman, R.(2001a) Human Sexuality: Answers from Evolutionary Psychology. Journal of Evolutionary Psychology,22, 53-55.

Esposito, K. B., A., Barza,L, and Mellman,T. (1999). Evaluation of dream content in combat-related PTSD. *Journal of Traumatic Stress, 12*(4), 681-687.

Fenchel, G. (1998). Exquisite Intimacy—Dangerous Love. *Issues in Psychoanalytic Psychology, 20*(1), 17-27.

Fenchel, G. H. E. (1998). *The Mother—Daughter Relationship Echoes Through Time.*: Jason Aronson Inc. Northvale, New Jersey.

Fenchel, G. (2005). What is Love? *Issues in Psychoanalytic Psychology, 27*(1), 49-67.

Fisher, H. (2000). Lust, attraction, attachment: Biology and evolution of the three primary emotion systems for mating, reproduction, and parenting. *Journal of Sex Education & Therapy.*, 25(1), 96-104.

Foa, U. G., Foa, E.B. (1974). *Societal Structures of the Mind.*: Charles C Thomas. Illinois.

Foehrenbach, L. M., Lane, R.C. (1994). An object relational approach to resistance: The use of aggression as a barrier to love. *Psychotherapy in Private Practice, 13*(3), 23-42.

Fonagy, P.; Gergely, G.; Jurist, E.L.; Target, M. (2002). *Affect Regulation, Mentalization and the Development of the Self.*: Other Press. NY.

Freud, S. (1910a). A Special Type of Object Made By Men. In E. Jones. (Ed.), *In Collected Papers Vol.IV* (pp. 192-202).

Freud, S. (1912). The most prevalent form of degradation in erotic life. In E. Jones (Ed.), *Collected Papers In No. 10 Vol.IV*: The Hogarth Press and the Institute of Psycho-analysis. London 1950.

Freud, S. (1914/1957). On Narcissism: An Introduction. In *Standard Edition. Part XIV* (pp. 73-102): London: Hogarth Press.

Freud, S. (1966). The psychopathology of everyday life. New York, Norton.

Gardner, R. A. (1987). The parental alienation syndrome and the differentiation between fabricated and genuine child abuse: Creative Therapeutics. Cresskill, New Jersey.

Geraskov, E. A. (1994). The internal contradiction and the unconscious sources of activity. *Journal of Psychology.*, 128(6), 625-634.

Gordon, R. M. (1975). *Effects of interpersonal and economic resources upon values and the quality of life.*: Dissertation Abstracts International.

Gordon, R. M. (1982). Systems-object relations view of marital therapy: Revenge and reraising. In L. R. A. Wolberg, M. (Ed.), *Group and Family Therapy.*: Brunner-Mazel.

Gordon, R. M. (1997). Handling Transference and Countertransference Issues with the Difficult Patient. *The Pennsylvania Psychologist, 18*(3), 147-149.

Gordon, R.M. (1998).The Medea Complex and the Parental Alienation Syndrome: When Mothers Damage Their Daughter's Ability to Love a Man. In Gerd Fenchel Ed. *The Mother-Daughter Relationship Echoes Through Time.*Jason Aronson Inc. Northvale, New Jersey.

Gordon, R. M. (2001). MMPI/MMPI-2 Changes in Long-Term Psychoanalytic Psychotherapy. *Issues in Psychoanalytic Psychology, 23*(1), 59-79.

Gordon, R. M. (2002). *Child Custody Evaluators: Psychologists or Detectives?* In: Pennsylvania Bar Institute, Mechanicsburg, Pa.

Guntrip, H. (1969). *Schizoid Phenomena, Object relations and the Self.*: New York:International Universities Press.

Hartman, E. a. B., R. (2003). Dream Imagery becomes more intense after 9/11/01. *Dreaming, 13*(2), 61-66.

Harvey, J. H. (1989). People's naïve understandings of their close relationships: Attributional and personal construct perspectives. *International Journal of Personal Construct psychology., 2*(1), 37-48.

Hoglend, P. E., Vibeke; Sorbye, Oystein; Heyerdahl, Oscar; et al. (1994). The role of insight in exploratory psychodynamic psychotherapy. *British Journal of Medical Psychology, 67*(4), 305-317.

Horn, J. (1976). Love: The Most Important Ingredient in Happiness. *Psychology Today, 10*(2), 98-102.

Howard, K. I., Moras, K., Brill, P. L., Martinovich, Z., & Lutz, W. (1996). Evaluation of psychotherapy. Efficacy, effectiveness, and patient progress. *American Psychologist, 51*(10), 1059-1064.

Jacobson, E. (1971). *Depression: Comparative Studies of Normal, Neurotic, and Psychotic Conditions.*: International Universities Press, Inc. New York.

Kernberg, O. F. (1974). Barriers to falling and remaining in love. *Journal of the American Psychoanalytic Association., 22*, 486-511.

Kernberg, O. F. (1975). *Borderline conditions and pathological narcissism.* New York: J. Aronson.

Kernberg, O. F. (1976). *Object-relations theory and clinical psychoanalysis.* New York: J. Aronson.

Kernberg, O. F. (1980). *Internal world and external reality : object relations theory applied.* New York: J. Aronson.

Kernberg, O. F. (1985). *Borderline conditions and pathological narcissism.* New York: J. Aronson : Distributed by Scribner.

Kernberg, O. F. (1992). *Aggression in personality disorders and perversions.* New Haven: Yale University Press.

Kernberg, O. F. (1995). *Love relations : normality and pathology.* New Haven: Yale University Press.

Kernberg, O. F. (2002). *Borderline conditions and pathological narcissism* (Expanded ed.). Northvale, NJ: Jason Aronson.

Kernberg, O. F. (2004). *Aggressivity, narcissism, and self-destructiveness in the psychotherapeutic relationship: new developments in the psychopathology and psychotherapy of severe personality disorders*. New Haven: Yale University Press.

Kohut, H. (1966). Forms and transformations of narcissism. *J Am Psychoanal Assoc, 14*(2), 243-272.

Kohut, H. (1971). *The analysis of the self; a systematic approach to the psychoanalytic treatment of narcissistic personality disorders*. New York,: International Universities Press.

Kohut, H., Goldberg, A., & Stepansky, P. E. (1984). *How does analysis cure?* Chicago: University of Chicago Press.

Langs, R. (1983). *Unconscious Communication in Everyday Life.*: Jason Aronson,Inc. New York and London.

Loftus, E.F. and Hoffman, H.G. (1989). Misinformation and memory: The creation of new memories. *Journal of Experimental Psychology: General, 118*, 100-104.

Luepnitz, D. A. (2002). *Schopenhauer's porcupines: Intimacy and its dilemmas: Five stories of psychotherapy*. New York, NY, US: Basic Books.

Mahler, M. (1974). Symbiosis and Individuation: The psychological birth of the human infant. In *The Psychological Study of the Child*. (Vol. 29, pp. 98-106).

McCarthy, G. and Taylor, A. (1999). Avoidant/ambivalent attachment style as a mediator between abusive childhood experiences and adult relationship difficulties. *Journal of Child Psychology and Psychiatry and Allied Disciplines, 40*(3), 465-477.

McWilliams, N. (1994). *Psychoanalytic Diagnosis Understanding*

Personality Structure in the Clinical Process.: Guilford Press. New York.

McWilliams, N. (1999). *Psychoanalytic Case Formulation*: Guilford Press, N.Y.

Meston, C. and Frohlich, P.F. (2003). Love at first fright: Partner salience moderates roller-coaster induced excitation transfer. *Archives of Sexual Behavior., 32*(6), 537-544.

Monsen, J., Odland, T., Faugli, A., Daae, E., et al. (1995). Personality disorders and psychosocial changes after intensive psychotherapy: A prospective follow-up of an outpatient psychotherapy project, 5 years after end of treatment. *Scandinavian Journal of Psychology., 36*(3), 256-268.

Motley, M. T. (1985). Slips of the tongue. *Scientific American., 253*(3), 116-127.

Mulkens, S.; de Jong,P. and Merckelbach, H. (1996). Disgust and spider phobia. *Journal of Abnormal Psychology, 105*(3), 464-468.

Murray, G. W., Hay, D. A., & Armstrong, S. M. (1995). Personality factors in seasonal affective disorder: Is seasonality an aspect of neuroticism? *Personality & Individual Differences, 19*(5), 613-617.

Pao, P. (1973). On defensive flight to a new object. *International Journal of Psychoanalytic Psychotherapy., 2*(3), 230-337.

Pines, Ayala Malach (1999) Falling in Love: Why We Choose the Lovers We Choose. Routledge New York.

Pope,K. and Tabachnick,B.G.. (1994). Therapists as patients: A national survey of psychologists' experiences, problems, and beliefs. *Professional Psychology: Research & Practice, 25*(3), 247-258.

Richard, L. S., Wakefield, J.A. and Lewak, R. (1990). Similarity of personality variables as predictor of martial satisfaction: Minnesota Multiple Personality Inventory (MMPI) item analysis. *Personality and Individual Differences, 11*, 39-43.

Schore, A. N. (1994). *Affect Regulation and the Origin of the Self: The Neurobiology of Emotional Development*: Lawrence Erlbaum Assoc. New Jersey.

Schore, A.N. (2003) *Affect Dysregulation and Disorders of the Self.* W.W. Norton & Co. New York.

Shaver, P.R. and Clark, C.L.. (1994). The Psychodynamics of Adult Romantic Attachment. In J. M. M. a. R. F. Bornstein (Ed.), *Empirical Perspectives on Object Relations Theory.* (pp. 105-156.): American Psychological Association.

Sperling, M. B. (1987). Ego identity and desperate love. *Journal of Personality Assessment, 51*(4), 600-605.

Stephan, W.A.; Berscheid, E. and Walster, E. (1971). Sexual arousal and interpersonal perception. *Journal of Personality and Social Psychology, 20*, 93-101.

Stern, H. R. (1978). *The Couch: Its use and meaning in psychotherapy*: Human sciences Press. New York. N.Y.

Sternberg, R. J. (1986a). A triangular theory of love. *Psychological Review, 93*, 119-135.

Sternberg, R. J. (1999). *Love Is A Story: A New Theory of Relationships*: Oxford University Press, England.

Stoller, R. (1979). *Sexual Excitement*: New York: Patheon.

Tennov, D. (1979). *Love and Limerence: The Experience of Being in Love*: New York: Stein and Day.

Walters, E. M., S.; Treboux, D.; Crowell, J. and Albersheim, L. (2000). " (2000). Attachment Security in Infancy and Early Adulthood: A Twenty-Year Longitudinal Study. *Child Development, 71*(3), 684-689.

Wampold, B. E. (2001). *The great psychotherapy debate: Models, methods, and findings.*: Mahwah, NJ: Lawrence Erlbaum.

Williams,D. and Schill,T. (1994). Adult attachment, love styles and self defeating personality characteristics. *Psychological Reports, 75*(1), 31-34.

Winch, R. (1958). *Mate Selection: A Study of Complementary Needs.*: New York: Harper and Row.

Winnicott, D. W. (1960). Ego Distortion in Terms of the True and False Self. In. *In The Maturational Processes and the Facilitating Environment.1965.*: London: Hogarth Press; Toronto: Clarke, Irwin and Co. Ltd.

Young, A. (1997). Finding the mind's construction in the face. *Psychologist., 10*(10), 447-452.

Ziv, A. (1993). *Psychology: The Science of Understanding Human Beings.(Hebrew)*: Tel Aviv: Am Oved. Cited in Ayala Malach Pines (1999) Falling in Love: Why We Choose the Lovers We Choose. Routledge New York.

10 CE Credits of American Psychological Association Continuing Education Credits for Psychologists

The Institute for Advanced Psychological Training is an organization approved by the American Psychological Association to offer continuing education for psychologists. The Institute for Advanced Psychological Training maintains responsibility for the program.

Educational Objectives: Learn—What is romantic love, why does it often not last, what are the love disturbances and how does one recognize them and what does one do about them?

This home study course will provide 10 CE hours of APA approved credits. This home study course is intended for any psychologist wishing to be more informed about healthy and unhealthy love relations as a reference for research or for therapeutic work with patients.

No refunds can be offered after the purchase of this book and CE credit offer. A CE certificate will be given to you upon a 70% or better score. You may take the CE exam as often as you wish until you achieve at least a passing score.

Go to WWW.MMPI-INFO.COM and then to Continuing Education. Email questions to MMPI@enter.net

CE Test Questions:

1. What are Ziv's four stages of romantic love?

2. According to Otto Kernberg what are the two love disturbances often found with the Narcisstic and Borderline Personalities?

3. What are the other three love disturbances added by Salman Akhtar?

4. What percent of young adults had the same secure verses insecure attachment classification in their current intimate relationships as they had 20 years earlier as infants with their mothers?

5. Freud in 1912 said that, "To ensure a fully normal attitude in love..." the sensual feelings must unite with what other feelings?

6. According to Robert Sternberg what are the three components of consummate love?

7. Helen Fisher found that humans and other mammals have evolved three primary emotion systems that combine for love. What are they?

8. What are the five main contributing factors in Gordon's integrated meta-theory of love relations?

9. According to Kernberg what is the basis of idealization at the primitive level of personality structure?

10. According to Gordon an intimacy can promote personal growth when it has what components?

11. Individuals with a Borderline Personality Structure may swing between idealization and devaluation in their love relationships because of their poor capacity for normal:

12. According to Gordon's research it took at least how many years in psychoanalytic psychotherapy to begin to go deep enough for personal growth and a better ability to love?

About the Author

Robert M. Gordon, Ph.D. ABPP is a Diplomate of Clinical Psychology and a Fellow of the Division of Psychoanalysis and served on the Governing Body of the American Psychological Association. He served as President of the Pennsylvania Psychological Association and received its Distinguished Service Award. He authored of over 30 scholarly journal articles and book chapters. He has a private practice in Allentown, Pennsylvania specializing in psychoanalytic psychotherapy, forensic psychology and MMPI-2 research and workshops.

WWW.MMPI-INFO.COM